PRAISE FOR
YOUR BRAIN IS A SAFE SPACE

"Rosenthal encourages others with the disorder to use the lessons and tools that she says turned her life around. This is a cheerleading, you-can-do-it kind of book, with step-by-step lifestyle modifications."

—Nancy Szokan, *The Washington Post*

"Recovery from PTSD is finally possible. This is not just a book to help you get past your trauma, it will also help you fully heal from it and get over it."

—Mark Goulston, MD, author of *Post-Traumatic Stress Disorder for Dummies* and *Just Listen*

"An ideal workbook for trauma survivors to use in their journey to emotional health."

—Robert Scaer, MD, author of *The Trauma Spectrum*

"With empowering suggestions and her own wealth of expertise, Rosenthal provides the resources that can help with PTSD recovery. From mindfulness to meditation, Rosenthal shares a wealth of knowledge that could be helpful to anyone in any stage of recovery from PTSD, as well as to professionals looking to broaden their knowledge base and find new treatment techniques."

—Clarie Foster, *Foreword Reviews*

YOUR BRAIN IS A SAFE SPACE

OTHER BOOKS BY
MICHELE ROSENTHAL

Before the World Intruded: Conquering the Past and Creating the Future, A Memoir

Your Life After Trauma: Powerful Practices to Reclaim Your Identity

YOUR BRAIN IS A SAFE SPACE

HOW TO HEAL TRAUMA AND PTSD

MICHELE ROSENTHAL

Conari
Press

CORAL GABLES, FL

Cover, Layout & Design: Megan Werner
Cover Photo/illustration: Marina / stock.adobe.com

For permission requests, please contact the publisher at:
Mango Publishing Group
2850 S Douglas Road, 2nd Floor
Coral Gables, FL 33134 USA
info@mango.bz

For special orders, quantity sales, course adoptions and corporate sales, please email the publisher at sales@mango.bz. For trade and wholesale sales, please contact Ingram Publisher Services at customer.service@ingramcontent.com or +1.800.509.4887.

Your Brain Is A Safe Space: How to Stop Trauma and PTSD from Controllling Your Life

Library of Congress Cataloging-in-Publication number: 2022952095
ISBN: (pb) 978-1-68481-187-8 (hc) 978-1-68481-282-0 (e) 978-1-68481-188-5
BISAC category code: PSY049000, PSYCHOLOGY / Psychopathology / Depression

*For you, in honor of your willingness to hope,
your openness to change, your desire to be free.*

TABLE OF CONTENTS

FOREWORD

There are many approaches to treating the multiple faces of trauma. Because traumatic impacts are so individualized, a one-size-fits-all approach does not allow for treating those personal short- and long-term impacts in ways designed for each person's needs and circumstances. Recent changes to the recognized definition of post-traumatic stress disorder in the *Diagnostic and Statistical Manual of Mental Disorders* (DSM-5) have modified what constitutes a traumatic stressor to include "exposure to actual or threatened death, serious injury, or sexual violence" through direct experience, witnessing, learning that the victim is a family member or friend, or repeated exposure to traumatic details through work.

As Rosenthal aptly states, having knowledge about trauma and PTSD empowers and helps those who have been traumatized to begin and follow through on their recovery journeys. One important component of knowledge is the mind-body connection. This interaction of mind and body means that traumatic events exist beyond the time in which they occurred, not only in memory and emotion, but also in brain structures (hippocampus, amygdala) and body reactions. In her book *Molecules of Emotion*, Candace Pert states that the emotions engendered by trauma are held in the cellular structure of the self. Rosenthal does an excellent job describing brain structures in the "head brain" as well as long-term impacts. She reinforces the scientific findings that trauma impacts the hippocampus in its attempts to process, consolidate, and store traumatic memories in ways that may produce hippocampal shrinkage and atrophy, as well as amygdala growth, as emotions and intrusive symptoms take over. One major truth presented in this book, however, is that these impacts are not necessarily—nor do they have to remain—static. The brain is plastic and can remodify itself. However, the first requirement for change is the desire to change. Committing to change and recovery is a major step in re-creating the self.

Lying behind this process of re-creation is the recognition that there are five major psychological needs, each of which has accompanying belief structures relating to the self, others, and the world. As Rosenbloom and Williams (2010) wrote, these five needs of safety, trust, power/control, esteem, and intimacy are core self structures that are impacted by traumatic events and may appear to be permanently changed. Some researchers believe that changing those negative, altered beliefs is difficult, if not impossible; however, another key truth in *Your Brain Is a Safe Space* is that working with and challenging those beliefs, often through the substitution of more positive ones, is a key to healing.

An individual must truly want to change if any change is to occur. Keys to healing revolve around the five psychological needs, whether presented in their developmental order or as specific parts of healing. Rosenthal says "your beliefs drive 100 percent of your behavior" (page 101). Many of the statements in this book illustrate this healing process.

SAFETY:

- Restoring your identity after being traumatized "leads to a grounded sense of safety" (page 141).

- Safety comes from things you can depend on (page 196).

TRUST:

- Trust the process of healing. There are many truths in this workbook that will guide you through that process.

- Trusting yourself is a learnable skill (page 117).

POWER/CONTROL:

- Challenging emotions and maintaining control over them is powerful as you challenge your mind to hold emotions inside that are positive and negative. One emotion ultimately wins.

- You cannot change what happened to you, but you can change how you function in the present and future as you "choose to define who you are" (page 139).

ESTEEM:

- Your sense of self-worth begins with believing you matter (page 99).

- Higher self-esteem can regulate emotional distress (page 99).

- It is important to identify what you are good at and then do it often (page 100).

INTIMACY:

- Connection and reconnection (with self, mind/body, others, and your world) is necessary for healing.

In conclusion, Rosenthal reminds the reader in many ways that challenging beliefs (and hopefully changing the destructive ones) is one of the most important aspects of healing from a traumatic event or events that has changed the survivor. In other words, "your beliefs are who you are" (page 174) and "[your] beliefs create your world" (page 150). Choose to do! Choose to move forward! Ask yourself what Michele Rosenthal terms the one primary question to ask yourself in recovery: "What's one small thing I can do today?" (page 115).

—**Mary Beth Williams, PhD, LCSW**

INTRODUCTION

There are several elements that make post-traumatic stress disorder (PTSD) recovery enormously challenging; this is a book about making it easier. The safer and more in control you feel—over your own internal experience—the safer and more in control you'll be as you examine how, when, and in what way to move toward recovery. This means developing a vision for healing, understanding the effects of trauma, identifying an approach to change, and refining a system for reconnecting to the authentic you, plus establishing ways to handle a variety of recovery obstacles from an attitude of strength, resilience, commitment, and determination.

Many survivors (including me during my own PTSD recovery) search for the "magic bullet"—the one thing that will erase the pain, fear, discomfort, and disconnection that PTSD creates and that some parts of healing actually amplify. This is a reasonable quest, as the life-crushing effects of PTSD would make anyone thirst for immediate freedom. Of course, there is no quick solution. Even though you'll learn many strategies in the following pages, they are not meant to offer miraculous solutions. Instead, they are designed to build a flexible and adaptive system that strengthens your approach to healing so that you ultimately achieve your recovery vision.

A successful "healing rampage," as I affectionately called my PTSD recovery process, is about exploring and discovering how to make the shift from power*less* (the definition of the PTSD mindset) to power*ful*, the definition of a survivor who reassumes her place in the world by making choices and taking actions in alignment with her desires for experiencing a fulfilling life and self. If you want to connect to a sense of your own power, learn how to create more effective coping and healing processes and reclaim control over who you are and how you live, then the small, manageable actions included with each strategy will help you become one of the thousands who move through PTSD and come out the other side stronger, more effective, capable, and living a life that feels good.

On the other hand, if you're in the mood to stay stagnant, hold onto beliefs like "I'm damaged and can't be helped!" want to live the rest of your life defined by PTSD, or wish to hold onto trauma and the idea that PTSD is a life sentence, then I'll tell you right now: this book will disappoint you. To do all of those un-healing things, you don't need a book; you simply need to give in to the PTSD depression, hopelessness, helplessness, and anxiety. In this case it would be wise for you to set down this book and pick it up again on a day when you feel like getting out of that space, which is entirely possible when you work the suggested strategies and make them your own.

I know the PTSD recovery process intimately because, for more than twenty-five years (starting at the age of thirteen), I struggled with PTSD symptoms and the chore of living a life despite them. When I finally entered recovery in my thirties, I threw myself full-force into studying the literature of PTSD, as well as psychological theories of healing trauma all the way back to the 1800s. I was determined to crack the code of both understanding and healing. It took several years and treatment modalities for me to reach where I am today: 100 percent free of symptoms for nearly a decade despite significantly severe triggers.

By the time my recovery was complete, I had amassed an enormous wealth of information and desired to give back so that others would have access to knowledge that had been so useful in my healing success. This impulse led me to host the radio program *Changing Direction* (on which I've interviewed over 150 experts about trauma and PTSD recovery); launch the Heal My PTSD forum (join us, it's free at HealthUnlocked.com/HealMyPTSD); write *Before the World Intruded: Conquering the Past and Creating the Future*, an award-nominated case study in trauma, PTSD, and successful recovery, plus *Your Life After Trauma: Powerful Practices to Reclaim Your Identity*, a step-by-step program for answering the question, "Who am I now?" I also became a certified professional coach trained in alternative modalities that facilitate healing. Through all of these activities, I've worked to distill the essence of the PTSD experience and identify what successful healing universally requires. Most importantly, I've focused on how to personalize the process for your own success. In this book, I've chunked down all of this information into bite-size pieces in five essential categories to help you learn, strengthen, and create choices and actions that increase flexibility and resolve conflicts so that you might experience forward momentum.

There are two ways to strategize your approach to this book:

1. Read straight through from beginning to end and allow the subjects to slowly move you through a course of orientation and action.

2. Examine the table of contents and dip into each section according to what you need on any given day.

However you read, allow yourself the time, space, and opportunity to try one suggested action at a time. Employ self-care techniques to feel safe and in control; immediately stop any exercise that seems triggering or for which you do not feel ready. You can use any of the strategies on your own or in collaboration with a trauma-trained professional. As you read through this book, you might want a notebook or journal in which to collect your thoughts, responses to the exercises, and other material. Or you might open a new folder on your computer. Having a record will let you see how far you've evolved and can also help you organize effective strategies for future use. Lastly, read this book as if we are together: It's me talking to and with you—survivor to survivor, coach to client, friend to friend. We're in this together every step of the way.

PTSD becomes a lifestyle; so does healing. Nothing works for everyone. Your mission in this book (as in all of your PTSD recovery) is to find the strategies that work for you and work them every day. You'll notice certain themes running throughout all of the subjects: the importance of beliefs, the necessity of pacing, the role of self-kindness, the benefits of joy and play, and the development of intuition, to name a few. When you see a theme, pay special attention: Themes are foundational elements from which all of your success will evolve.

Ongoing advancements in the field of neuroscience prove the brain's capacity for continual change, which means the possibility for healing exists for you in every moment. If you feel ready to reclaim the power trauma stole from you and change your life one moment at a time, then turn the page. Gently allow yourself to begin creating the New You while designing a healing strategy that allows you to embody a sensation of calm, confidence, and control.

You have enormous healing potential; the goal is learning to access it. You can do this. Dig deep. I believe in you!

PART ONE

YOU CAN HEAL

It's a generally accepted fact that the key to achieving anything is being able to visualize it. The reason for this has a lot to do with how the brain works: The more it knows, understands, and "sees" what you want, the more efficiently, effectively, and effortlessly it helps you create what you want. This is exactly why having a healing vision—for both how healing happens and how you can begin to create it—becomes so important in the PTSD recovery process.

Approach the following pages as your introduction to ideas that make recovery eminently possible, plus ways you can create, embody, and engage with a healing vision of your very own. The more you clarify and then learn to step into the world you want, the more success you will achieve in reducing PTSD symptoms and reclaiming a self and life you love.

HOW HEALING BEGINS

Healing begins with hope.

At this moment you may question how possible it is to reach your healing objectives. There will (often) be moments of doubt—that's all right. There's still room for hope.

The good news is you don't have to know exactly *how* you're going to succeed in your quest. Having hope just means putting out there that you desire to achieve the outcome you seek.

In moments of doubt, you can hold onto hope by saying to yourself, "I'm open to the idea that it's possible for me to..."

Having hope increases strength when you're clear about what you hope for. Today, outline what you hope for in terms of:

- your life
- who you are
- your recovery

- your relationships with others
- your experience in the world
- your future

In your notebook, journal, or computer, complete this statement: "I hope..."

~~~~~

If you're wondering whether it's possible to feel better, the answer is emphatically, yes!

While friends and family may have advised you to "just get over it," you've probably encountered difficulty in doing so. There's a very scientific reason for why the "just get over it" recovery method doesn't work: Your behaviors are embedded in neural pathways in your brain, in the very biology of your nervous system. Literally, the traumatic experience has become a part of you, which means you can "just get over it" about as easily as you can get over infected tonsils.

As with your tonsils, healing after trauma means tending to what's wrong. In this case, that involves rewiring and retraining your brain. Since your brain rewires and retrains itself all the time, it's very adept at utilizing these skills. Your role in recovery is to specifically apply these skills in areas related to trauma. Essentially, you are your brain's guide through the maze of trauma recovery. Your mission is to (1) identify what your brain needs in order to rewire the trauma pathways and then (2) develop a protocol for creating the retraining that will achieve the desired results.

> If you were going to teach your brain something new about post-trauma life, what would it be? What kind of repetitive experience could you develop that would offer your brain opportunities to learn that idea?

~~~~~~

Bringing yourself to a place of peaceful healing means repairing the bridges that were blown up in yourself and your world when trauma occurred.

In his song "In Repair," John Mayer croons, "So much to do to set my heart right." (If you don't know that song, go listen to it or watch the video; it's a great recovery anthem.) This sentiment so aptly describes where a great deal of the pain comes from in the PTSD experience.

In the post-trauma identity crisis that accompanies PTSD, you question how to define yourself, wonder what's true and what's false, and lack a sense of what's right for you—these are heart and/or soul wounds. One way to answer the questions and refill that sense of rightfulness is to engage in repair of the things that feel most devastated.

What are those things for you? Take some time to sit in a quiet space, peer into your heart, and see what's most damaged—what most needs to be repaired. Fixing those things will bridge you to the next phase of healing.

Then choose a recovery anthem and play it daily. Tweet the song title and/or lyrics to @ChangeYouChoose, #healmyptsd.

~~~~

Healing requires recalibration, which is the careful process of bringing things back into scale, a place of neutrality.

PTSD living happens in a place of extremes: anxiety, panic, depression, loneliness, grief, loss, sadness, despair, and [insert your ideas here]. It's a little like living on the edge of an abyss, feeling that any moment you'll teeter into open space.

Successful coping and healing bring you back from the edge of the abyss and get your feet onto more firm ground, from where you can see into the chasm but have removed the danger of falling into it.

The success of recalibration relies on getting things back into a state of equilibrium. If you were going to feel more neutral in one area of your life or coping today, what would you have to do?

~~~~

Healing is about recreating who you are and rebuilding your life.

The modus operandi (MO) of every survivor is to create an environment and sensation of being safe and in control. You're working very hard at doing that—which is why you're feeling such an enormous amount of stress.

Here's the big secret: Focusing on staying safe and being in control through rigid coping mechanisms doesn't create recovery. Healing is all about reversing the process in which you've come to live: learning to feel safe even when you don't have the ultimate control, and learning to be in control even when you don't feel safe.

Consider this new MO: You have choices to make. Decide what changes you want to experience, then take actions to achieve them. After that, let loose all of your planning. Stay in the moment and respond to what you experience.

> In the avoidance perspective of post-trauma life, your motivation is to move away. You avoid threat by skirting it. However, you can't go into your future by stepping back or to the side. The future, since it exists in front of you, can be fully entered only by moving straight toward it. What is right in front of you on the road to recovery? What does that require you to do? Record your responses in your notebook, journal, or computer.

Healing means making better choices and taking more effective actions over a long period of time.

If you do this, eventually you will have installed in yourself an entirely new system for operating in the world. The foundation for this new system is the thoughts, beliefs, choices, and actions that emerge from your deeply connected sense of self. Cultivating the strong, confident, connected, and capable you is like honing the keel of a boat: It gives you balance and a way to choose and control your direction.

In the end, post-traumatic stress disorder recovery isn't just about being able to face the past; it's also about being able to connect to the present and envision a future. That begins with a connection to yourself.

Pause for a moment and notice how disconnected from yourself you feel. Do you feel disconnected from your mind, body, creativity, skills, or pleasures? In what way does that show up?

In your notebook, journal, or computer, create a two-column chart. In the column on the left, list all the ways you feel disconnected. Next, imagine that by the end of this year, these connections will have been restored. In the column on the right, fill in what will have to happen for you to feel reconnected in those areas.

~~~~~

Making choices and taking actions—sometimes before you even believe in the possibilities of the outcome—will naturally evolve your confidence and perceptions.

The tendency is to think you have to feel the truth of your healing possibilities before you can move toward them. So false!

Possibility exists for you in every moment, regardless of whether or not you feel its presence. All you need in order to inch ahead is to be able to do any or all of the following:

1. *Hope* that things can change

2. *Imagine* a different way of living

3. *Wish* a better life exists for you

4. *Want* your circumstances to transform

5. *Embrace* the idea, "It can happen for me."

The truth of who you are and what your life is really about constantly changes. Pick one of the preceding options and carry it with you today. See how much you can incorporate it into your thought process.

Today you are your trauma self, but your post-trauma self waits to be discovered.

A key feature of PTSD is powerlessness. For example, you feel powerless:

- in the midst of your trauma
- in the midst of your mind after trauma
- over psychological symptoms
- over physical symptoms
- in controlling the healing process
- about finding help in the healing process
- about who you've become despite who you used to be

In healing, you will learn to take back the power trauma stole from you. How do you do this? A (powerful) first step can be found in constructing your post-trauma identity.

Your post-trauma identity redefines you as someone for whom trauma occurred in the past but who is no longer negatively driven by trauma in the present. That full identity will include personality traits, dreams, and a vision for living a future that is full of meaningful and productive experiences.

It's okay if all of this seems foreign and/or unattainable right now. Today, open your mind to the possibility that, someday, you will shift into a post-trauma identity whose foundation is one of power, strength, homeostasis, and "I can handle it!" thinking.

Losing what you did due to trauma is very meaningful. That loss demands attention and deserves it.

Over the course of life, you lose many things...from house keys to favorite sweaters, books, and scraps of paper with important information. You don't, however, keenly feel the loss or become blindingly infuriated by it. While you may have a momentary pang of regret, the loss of these types of things doesn't usually cause you to cry, feel physically ill, fall into a bout of despair, or become enraged.

How are those losses different from trauma? Those elements didn't define you; losing them didn't challenge your view of yourself, others, or the world.

Losing what you have because of trauma, however, does all of those things. Loss deserves recognition. Mourning that loss is a necessary component of healing.

What have you lost due to trauma? Make a list of everything you can think of and then put a star next to the losses that most bother you. Address these areas to begin your mourning process.

~~~~

Plan. Commit. Act. Heal.

You are a powerful being. Every day you endure symptoms that would drive another person insane. Still, you look for relief. You move through your days doing the best you can.

More and more often, you are able to make a difference for yourself when you practice what it means to make a choice and take an action. The survivors who heal PTSD are the ones who find ways to sustain this process for as long as it takes and despite every unexpected outcome or perceived setback.

You are capable of handling tough things with strength and resilience.

On a scale of 1 to 10 (10 being "I accept that completely!"), where do you rate your response to that idea? What would it take for you to move up one notch? How can you create a situation that encourages that to happen?

Be responsible and accountable.

What makes you feel responsible for executing the recovery you're attempting?

If you've ever tried to hold yourself accountable, you know how tough it can be. Different parts of you start having a conversation.

The part that wants you to follow through starts sounding like a cross parent, and the part that doesn't feel like doing the work sounds like a whiny child. As it does in real life, this kind of conversation can go around and around until you're both exhausted and nothing gets done.

Being held accountable finds real strength in its external origin. To an outside person less swayed by your whiny child part, you cannot fuss about what you do or don't want to do; you can follow through only because that's what is expected. If this scenario sounds more like a sergeant than a buddy, that's okay. If a buddy would let you get away with months of inertia, then it's a sergeant you need on your team!

Consider all the people you know whom you trust. Who wants you to succeed in your mission for healing? Make a list. From this list, choose one (or more) person(s) to whom you can confide your tasks and objectives and who will hold you accountable for getting them done following the schedule of choices and actions you devise.

Healing requires you to give up control.

In an attempt to reclaim control after trauma, you have built a world in which you control as much as possible. While that's sensible, strong, and wise, you have also built yourself the prison in which you now live—a place where, the more you expend your energy on control, the more controlled you are by your own brain, mind, and body.

At this point, it isn't trauma that controls you: You—and your belief system (embedded in both your conscious and subconscious psychological and neurobiological processes)—control you. To feel better, you will be required to release all of the controlling behaviors you have implemented.

Make a list of the (obsessive and compulsive) controlling behaviors you employ on any given day. (If you can't identify them, ask your friends, family, or colleagues; they will happily tell you what they've noticed!) Choose one behavior that you feel comfortable working with, and imagine what it would take to gradually lessen and then release it. Write out the steps you imagine. Prioritize them and make an implementation plan.

~~~~~

Healing happens when you value who you are.

PTSD begins as an instinctive reaction to trauma but continues because your body and mind perpetuate the survival-mode cycle. The more you allow PTSD to continue, the more it builds on itself.

But you do have a choice. If you value yourself enough to believe you deserve to be well, then you can begin moving forward.

Today, ask yourself the following questions:

- Do I deserve to be free of PTSD symptoms?

- Do I deserve to live a joyful, productive, fulfilling life?

- Do I deserve to have peace of mind?

- Do I deserve to have a successful career?

- Do I deserve to have comforting, supportive, loving, and satisfying relationships?

On a scale of 1 to 10 (10 being "I am completely worthy!"), rate how worthy you feel of healing.

What would have to happen to increase that number up one notch on the scale? How can you do that? Who can help? Follow this process repeatedly until you reach the 8 to 10 range.

~~~~~~

Initially, healing can make PTSD symptoms worse.

You're overwhelmed by how difficult, scary, and out of control your mind, emotions, and the coping and recovery process feel. Sometimes you might even be afraid to let go of your survivor persona and coping techniques. As much as PTSD symptoms make your life miserable, they have become familiar: In the framework of post-traumatic stress symptoms, you recognize yourself, and this feels safe.

Healing, however, challenges you to let go of all that. Naturally, the unfamiliar is threatening and uncomfortable. To continue moving forward, you must develop a strong reserve of courage.

As you move toward healing, you must discover in yourself a sense of adventure and an attitude of fearlessness.

In what one area of recovery do you feel the most fear? If you were going to become fearless in that space, what would have to happen? How could you create one small step toward that outcome? Who can help?

~~~~~~

Lots of surprises happen throughout the trek to healing.

You'll surprise yourself with strength, courage, and fortitude. Your brain will surprise you with how it begins to function in new ways. Your emotions will surprise you with how they become more appropriate in the moment. Your mind will surprise you in how it learns to focus, synthesize, and integrate.

Look for the surprises, and then let them lead you forward into new territory. Where you are today may feel as if it has many questions. However, all of who you are today holds the answers.

> When you look back at how you've managed since your trauma(s), what surprises you about yourself? What skills or attitudes does this highlight about you? How can you use them in your healing process?

~~~~~

PTSD recovery has a very specific outcome.

What does recovery look like to you? Being able to achieve healing begins with clearly and specifically naming your desired result so that your brain begins formulating a successful process.

To better clarify your recovery, start working on your (very detailed and specific) answers to these questions:

- What do you wish to change about who you are today?

- How will you be different when your recovery is complete?

- How will you know when you have reached the end of your recovery?

> Repeatedly asking yourself these questions keeps you focused on the work of healing and creates a reality in which that healing begins to exist.

Trauma takes away your choices; recovery is about taking them back.

There is a you that exists transcendent of trauma. Taking back your power—redefining yourself outside trauma—is a process focused on becoming *who it is you really want to be* beyond and despite trauma. The ultimate mission is for the past to become a very tiny part of your very large, present self. Getting there includes going through these steps:

- Recognizing who you are in this moment

- Deciding what needs to be changed (this includes attitudes, perceptions, behaviors, beliefs)

- Developing a timeline

- Putting the plan into effect

- Defining who you want to become (professionally, personally, spiritually, etc.)

- Planning a series of actions

- Identifying objectives

Someday you're going to look back and marvel at the fact that you made it through PTSD to the other side. Today, imagine you have an ideal self, unaffected by trauma, who knows how to guide you there. Describe that person.

You are, in this moment, creating your own unique healing process.

The origin of how you think and feel, plus what you see (in terms of yourself, others, and the world), lies in your belief system. If you allow yourself to remain stagnant in an identity system that perpetuates negative beliefs about yourself and the world, then you will stay exactly where you are now.

The same goes for healing: You have many programmed beliefs about how healing is supposed to go. You may have thought, heard, or been told that you must:

- forgive
- talk
- remember
- forget

- release
- get over
- accept
- *(fill in the blank)*

The truth: There are zero prescriptions for how PTSD recovery will occur. Healing has zero set programs. What worked for one person may or may not bring you the same results. What one person believes is true about recovery may or may not be true for *your* recovery.

> You are a unique individual. Allow your healing efforts to reflect that. What do you hate about your current process? What would you prefer instead? Research your options for giving yourself what you want.

~~~~~~

Recovery success largely derives from your intention for how you will approach your healing transformation.

There are many ways to accomplish everything you want to do in recovery. Whether you're aware of it or not, you develop a healing action plan full of strategic processes. Once you make choices and take actions, you tweak the process depending on the feedback you receive from the results and outcomes.

For a long time, you (or others) have probably had expectations about how your recovery is supposed to go. Plus, what you "should" do, what the results "ought" to be, what length of time it "must" take, and, and, and...

If you listen to that language, it's not surprising if you don't make the progress you hope for. Such enormous focus on the should-ought-must ideas creates a huge amount of pressure that can make you so tired that even your muscles feel too heavy for your skeleton to carry.

In this way, expectations for recovery can be dangerous. *Expectations* are strong beliefs for how something will happen. They set the stage for disappointment, because you don't have exact control over how your recovery will occur. Unmet expectations can make you feel like a failure and bring on a big despair that you'll never be healed, all because you had this strong belief for how some future event would go—and then it didn't.

Healing in the confines of intractable beliefs is incredibly hard. Recovering in an environment that lacks flexibility is near to impossible. The perfect substitute for the weight of expectations: the power of purpose, otherwise known as *intention*.

An intention is an objective or a plan. It is a suggested course of action that states a mission or aim. Unlike the assumed outcomes held in the belief of an expectation, an intention merely *suggests the spirit* of how something will be approached. This allows the "how you will achieve it" to develop itself.

Throughout recovery, you have a choice in how you will approach any healing task. Rather than barreling into an activity at warp speed when you clearly define your intention prior to an action, you can slow down and ground your energy and action in the present spirit of showing up versus the future belief of how things will happen. Since intentions are all about how you choose to show up in and handle any moment, they offer an area in which you have 100 percent control.

Making the shift from expectation to intention is a conversion from seeking control over the "how" of your healing strategy (the exact steps and their outcomes) to the "what" of your vision (the way you will engage and be present).

Set your specific intention: How do you plan to engage in your recovery? What will that require?

What expectations do you have about your healing process? Get them out on the table right now! Make a list of what you believe is supposed to/will/must/ought/should/needs to happen in order for you to heal. Then check out the section "How to Gain (and Keep) Momentum" on page 107 for how to develop supportive intentions instead.

~~~~~

You are always on a path of personal discovery and exploration.

Notes from the path:

- The path is gloriously endless.

- If you hit a dead end, turn in a new direction; make a new start.

- Slowly, face all fear and discomfort; you can handle it.

- Find proactive ways to lessen fear before engaging in the work that needs to be done.

- The more empowered, confident, and secure you feel in your process, the more efficient and successful you will be.

- You have what it takes to feel better.

- Ideas, thoughts, and experiences that bring up the most intense emotions (both positive and negative) are signs from your deepest self about what is important to you.

- Pay attention to the signs; you can use them to more intentionally create both your recovery and your life.

- Care less about the recovery process itself and more about your intention for the end results.

While it may not always feel that way, there is plenty of room to contain any emotion sparked on the path. Imagine yourself as an ocean embodying the excess of any emotional spill.

CREATE YOUR PERSONAL HEALING STRATEGY

Because you are unique, your healing time will be individual to your own journey.

A popular recovery query is, "If I've struggled for X years, is healing still possible for me?" Many times the answer is yes. How long it will take for you to heal cannot be predicted or judged based on the details or facts of anyone else's process. Some survivors go from trauma to PTSD diagnosis to recovery in as little as six months. Others spend decades in the struggle before finding relief.

Factors that impact the length of recovery include your trauma history, willingness and readiness to engage and participate in the recovery process, plus feasibility (financial, physical, emotional), safe environment, and comfort level with the professionals, practices, modalities, and treatment approaches you utilize.

While the effects of trauma and PTSD become more embedded the longer they remain untended, the brain's willingness to change often opens the real possibility to reduce and even eliminate symptoms several years after their initial appearance.

Stop looking at others and focus on yourself. What conditions would help facilitate a consistent healing process for *you*? How can you create them?

Clarify, verify, strategize.

Clarity is being able to say, "I want..." The more specific and detailed a description you can use to fill in that blank, the more likely you will successfully devise a road map for healing.

When you *verify* something, you test its accuracy. Let's say you clarify that you want A. Verifying that means making sure it's true that you really do want that. Ask yourself, "Why do I want it?" If the answer feels right to you, then it's full steam ahead. If you don't have an answer, or if the answer comes back, "Hey, I don't really want that at all, because...!" then you know it's time to pull back and reassess.

When you *strategize,* you create an action plan. In this phase, you're asking yourself, "How am I going to do that?" This will be a multi-part answer, as you will need to outline and then prioritize and tweak several steps as you receive internal feedback along the way.

This is what the process of recovery is all about:

1. Know what you want.
2. Identify why you want it.
3. Outline the steps you need to take to get it.

Following those clues, you can move toward discovering your path to freedom.

> Take one aspect of your recovery and put it through the questions outlined here. Then decide what will be your first step or action and who (if anyone) can help you achieve that.

~~~~~

You always have the option to do something in the face of fear—or to not do it. Choose to do it.

The definition of courage is the ability to do something even though you are frightened.

Surviving your trauma required courage (resist the urge to dispute that statement—it is *true!*). Healing, too, requires courage. You are going to be asked to face tough things. You are going to experience intense emotions. You are strong enough to survive all of this.

While healing can sometimes seem more traumatic than your original trauma, you have what it takes to survive even the most devastating emotional crisis.

Think back to a time when you felt even just the tiniest bit of courage. What did that feel like? How did you access it? How might you access it again today?

~~~~~

Healing requires creativity and flexibility.

With any choice you make, the challenge is to combine all of the choices into a healing strategy that moves you toward feeling better, one choice at a time.

You can make the important choices highlighted here once, and then again and again as you and your recovery change, progress, stall, reset, and change again.

- **When to get help:** Your real chance to achieve positive results happens when you willingly engage in traditional and/or alternative therapeutic processes. Reach out for help when you're open to accepting it.

- **How much to participate in healing work:** You'll see results only if you put in the effort to do the work. At the same time, you alone know how much you're ready for and capable of doing; trust your internal responses to guide your activity.

- **Who, when, how, and whether to forgive:** Some say you must forgive first; others say you don't need to forgive at all. You know what's important to you in any given moment—trust what you feel you need.

- **Type of treatment modality:** There is more than one way to heal symptoms of PTSD. Do the research, then choose the process that most resonates with you—over and over until the job is done.

- **Velocity of the pace:** Everyone (including you) will want you to heal as soon as possible, but recovery requires a slow pace that allows your body and brain to make changes that stick. Choose a pace that allows you to feel comfortable with the work you're doing and able to adequately process and embody it.

- **Retrieval and recall:** You do not have to remember or vividly recall your trauma(s) in order to heal. Decide how much you need to/want to/can remember and work with that level.

Prior to making any decision, ask yourself, "How do I feel about this?" and then explore the "Why I feel this way is…" and "What I need right now is…" of your answers until a clear path appears to you.

~~~

No one can predict how long your recovery will take.

However, there are ways to assess whether or not the healing approach you're using is efficiently moving you forward.

A framework of assessment factors includes:

- **The nature of the trauma:** Rate how traumatic the event(s) feels on a scale of 1 to 10 (10 being the most traumatic). Depending on where you are in your recovery process, the higher the number, the more time it may take to achieve the ultimate results. Calibrate your expectations accordingly. Along the way, look for smaller clues that things are just a little bit better. To do this, rate your level of discomfort on the same scale, and chart the number weekly to see how it moves over a period of time.

- **Internal components that slow down the process:** The most relevant element in this area is fear. A treatment approach can work only as much as you're able to interact with it. If fear of the process or the material is high, then the process will happen more slowly. Smooth out this wrinkle by shifting your work to focus on the fear, plus any reluctance to heal. Then reapproach trauma-specific material.

- **External components that slow the process:** There are many well-intentioned but unskilled practitioners. For every modality, there are varying levels of training and educational programs. Part of your interview process when choosing the person you want to work with should incorporate asking in-depth questions about training. Equally important: The quality of your working relationship has an enormous effect on the results of the process. If you feel uncomfortable with the practitioner for any reason, then you will be less likely to fully engage in the protocol, and the modality won't work.

- **Your resonance level:** Because there are so many available healing modalities, you can absolutely find one that makes you feel comfortable. Check in with your resonance level (feeling on the right wavelength) with the modality you're using. You do your most successful work when you feel as comfortable as possible with the way you're approaching the work.

Different approaches will be appropriate for different phases of your recovery. When an approach doesn't yield positive results over a fair period of time, start looking for a different one. Shifting when necessary is one way to develop flexibility, which is a significant aspect of healing.

~~~~~

Sometimes, in order to feel better, you have to feel worse.

When you make choices about how you wish to change—and then act on them—it takes time for the results to be fully achieved. In this process, you have the choice to be motivated by one of two things:

1. Being *pushed* from behind to escape pain

2. Being *pulled* forward toward achieving pleasure

When you are pulled toward something, your propulsion system (the energy driving you) becomes much more positive and anabolic (rejuvenating) than when you allow yourself to be pushed.

You have the opportunity to choose: be pushed by the feel-bad past or be pulled by the feel-good possibility of the future.

Identify and envision the pain you are trying to escape. How does your desire to run away from it dictate your daily behavior?

Now identify and envision what you desire as the outcome of your PTSD recovery. How different would your day be if your behavior focused on moving toward this desire?

If you were going to shift your recovery propulsion system from avoiding pain to engaging with pleasure, what would that look like? What steps can you take to make that happen?

Trauma, memory, and behavior don't separate themselves. They are intertwined until you choose how they operate in your life.

Even after overcoming the effects of trauma, you will still have memories. Those memories can lead to both positive and negative behaviors. You always have a choice about how you respond to any moment: Will it be driven by trauma or not?

Rather than trying to separate trauma, memory, and behavior, try this instead: Decide how those elements can work together in your best interest. Seek to determine how to make your trauma experience, memories, and actions work to enhance how you live, what you do, how you experience today, and in what ways you achieve a life worth living.

What positive things do you now know about yourself, others, and the world? How is that knowledge useful? How can you apply it to the way you think, feel, behave, choose, and act today?

～～～

With PTSD symptoms, it's the norm to swing between rigidity and chaos.

Rigidity to bring a sense of control; chaos when all control goes out the window in an uncontrolled way.

While you're dealing with the back and forth of the pendulum, keeping balance is incredibly hard. And yet, balance is exactly what you need to bring life to a place of more synergy, safety, and solidity. Some places to think about doing this:

- **Body vs. mind:** How connected are you to your body? How much time do you spend solely in your mind? Being too far one way or the other can lead to more dissociation and less flexibility in responding to triggers, threats, and intense emotions.

- **Doing vs. relaxing:** If you are constantly on the go, then you keep your adrenaline high, which feeds anxiety, panic, and the feeling that things are out of control. Conversely, if you "relax" by mentally checking out for extended periods of time (that is, watching TV or playing video games), it becomes tough to feel engaged in your life.

- **Speaking vs. silence:** Trauma may have taught you that it's better to speak out, or it may have taught you it's safer to be quiet. In regular living, the truth is that there are times for both. Being aware of when you do and don't use your voice—and learning to do so appropriately—allows you to develop strength in reading situations, taking care of yourself, and engaging with others.

- **Control vs. lack of control:** Control is something you need to have as well as to let go of. The more control you develop (through those rigid coping mechanisms), the safer you will feel...until those coping mechanisms become tight as a tourniquet and cut off the blood flow of your life. The irony is that letting go of control actually puts you more in control than ever, particularly when you do it from an "I can handle it!" perspective.

- **Focus vs. lack of focus:** It's necessary to focus on how to, who will, and what it takes to aid your healing efforts. Also, you need downtime when your conscious mind can shift its focus to other (fun, engaging, entertaining) things so that your subconscious mind can mull, think, and create new solutions and action plans. Balancing how and when you focus can actually help you move forward faster, too, because it relieves pressure that increases anxiety and impedes healing.

Balance allows you to get closer to equilibrium. Which of the preceding areas resonates with you as a place where you could use some recalibration? Do one thing today that helps you move toward achieving that state.

In every part of PTSD recovery, you will be imperfect at implementing changes; that's absolutely okay.

In recovery, you are like a small child learning to walk: You figure out how to pull yourself upright, take a few wobbly steps, try to keep your balance, fall down and...get back up, knowing the only way to achieve the intended outcome is to keep trying and learning to do it better.

Similarly, healing PTSD is an act of conscious education and change combined with subconscious rewiring and rejuvenation. It's okay to make mistakes along the way; it's okay to feel as if you don't know what you're doing. It's also okay to try something and know you could do it better. All of that is part of the process of developing the New You.

Rather than criticize yourself for mistakes, take those moments as opportunities to prove you're on your own side. Being on your own team begins with something as simple as asking, "If I were going to be super-nice to me today, what would that look like?"

Ask yourself that now. Listen to the answers and follow through on embodying them.

Every "bad" behavior begins with a good intention.

In every minute, you are always doing the best you can. Even when you do something that is a "bad" behavior or leads to a bad outcome, it begins from a desire for something good.

Consider drug addicts: Negative addictive actions begin as the innocent desire to feel a positive emotion (e.g., peace, safety, comfort, relief).

When you recognize and acknowledge the good intention behind an unwanted behavior, you know where to refocus your actions: Perhaps you need to feel safer or more in control. Maybe you need to feel less stimulated or threatened. By shifting your perspective away from self-recrimination and toward creating the desired outcome, you focus more effectively on how to support the original good intention through healthy, deliberate, and positive actions.

When you become frustrated with your reactions and behaviors, take a moment to pause, step back, and assess: What's the good intention behind this behavior? Then identify a plan to bring yourself the wanted outcome through more productive actions.

You are the expert in *you*.

A resource person is one who has knowledge, skills, competence, and expertise in a given subject or area. Even during this confusing time, you know yourself better than anyone else. You know what you like and dislike; hate and fear; want and desire; desire and hope for. You know what you feel ready to do and what you feel completely uncomfortable even considering.

Today you are hereby appointed Chief Recovery Resource Person. Your duties include:

- being kind to yourself
- offering supportive guidance through uncomfortable moments
- discovering ways to access resilience
- identifying and engaging practices that bring recalibration
- dedicating time to research PTSD recovery
- committing to doing the work of healing
- developing a plan for creating post-traumatic growth
- creating self-care practices to support your well-being

Putting a resource person in charge means allowing a part of yourself to step forward and be the voice of strength, power, and certainty.

Imagine your PTSD self and your Resource self can talk. In the moments when you feel your PTSD self become unglued, engage your Resource self to provide ideas for what to do next in order to feel better.

The road back to self-connection is paved with intuition.

In life, you don't always have time to rationally and analytically think things through. In some moments, you need to just rely on the messages your mind and/or body send. Intuition is your ability to understand something without the need for conscious thought. You're born with this ability; it's a human trait, which means you still possess it, trauma or not. The problem is that, after a traumatic experience, it becomes difficult to trust anyone or anything—including yourself. Today, a disconnect exists between you and You. To be able to heal, you need to reconnect with your most intrinsic self—that intuitive self that, despite trauma's shock, still exists. Developing a practice of recognizing, tapping into, and heeding intuition puts you back in touch with the Good/Safe voice inside your head, which helps to balance out the Bad/Fear voice that trauma unleashed.

> You know your intuitive voice: It's the soft one you so often brush away. Since conscious thought can't qualify the advice of your intuitive voice, dismissing it is easy. Instead, develop a habit of connecting to intuition by listening to and acting on the advice of that voice in small, safe, and low-stress moments.

~~~~~~~~

Develop self-trust, self-efficacy, and a deep connection to your inner sense of knowing.

A call for action always accompanies intuition. Sometimes this means heeding the impulse to walk on the other side of the street, whereas other times it means reading a new book. Deferring to your intuition helps you develop a practice of following the feeling that feels most good, comfortable, and right—even when you can't explain why. In using both of the following intuition exercises, begin with small, inconsequential decisions. The first step is to gain a sense of comfortableness and trust. Once these elements are established, you can take the exercise to the next level by applying it to more consequential situations.

Use these steps to develop your "I trust my intuition!" process:

- **Step One: In moments of low stress, take some time to listen for that small inner voice.** What does it tell you? Give it a megaphone, turn up the volume, and then do what it says, no questions asked. For example, when you walk to work, the grocery store, or the mall, forget your usual path and allow your inner voice to decide what route you take. In this simple process, you give up control in a safe way to a part of you that transcends fearful and limited thinking and instead operates from a sense of security, safety, knowledge, and confidence. Fostering this inner connection is enormously healthy and beneficial to your future stability. For thirty consecutive days, develop your ability to trust this part and its ability to make good decisions.

- **Step Two: Amp up your body awareness.** Your body processes information and creates signals for you to interpret. By noticing how your body feels, you can increase your ability to make good decisions. To receive useful answers, the best questions to ask your body are yes/no questions. For example, ask "Should I go to this event?" Sometimes the answers from your body may be directly opposed to the ideas in your mind. For example, your mind may be full of jittery, "I am not in the mood to have dinner with my friends," while your body may be saying, "Go, it will be all right and you'll feel better." Conversely, your mind may know you must attend an event while your body says, "Don't go; I feel frightened!" This feedback clues you into what you need to do to successfully attend the event: Find a way to feel more safe and secure. If you form a partnership with it, your body can play a large role in delivering feelings that accurately point you in the right direction. Over the course of the next week, make seven decisions based on the information your body gives you.

Healing can come only when you let out the breath you're holding.

The main thrust of PTSD is living a life of fear. You feel anxious, tense, on guard, and ready for disaster in any moment. You do not feel safe—in the world or yourself. Healing begins when you imagine possibilities for an alternative way of living.

When you tap into your intuition, you open up a dialogue with your authentic self. Slowly, you awake from your emotional coma or the frozen tundra of your inner landscape. It's critical at this point for you to remember:

1. You always have choices.

2. You always have the right to choose (that is, how you live and feel and experience and recall).

Giving yourself the freedom to explore your choices and the possibilities that wait for you brings healing into the seat of your own determination.

> Exhale now and consider: What have you always wanted to do but have been told or thought you can't? Imagine that you free yourself to choose to do exactly that—how would it change who you are, how you feel, and how you live?

Recovery moves along, irritating and then surprising you in the most exciting, beautiful, and liberating ways.

Over time, PTSD symptoms (and other people) can make you feel that you are hopeless, that you will always live within the limits of symptoms. Then, after a lot of hard work, you will discover that you actually can change (in fact, your brain is hardwired for change). With diligent effort, it becomes apparent that those changes are limitless—that you are limitless.

Always remember: You are unique. The beliefs, thoughts, ideas, and emotions you bring to every moment influence those moments in wholly unpredictable ways. In lieu of certainty in the recovery process, develop certainty in how you show up for it.

> Today, make a promise to yourself about how you will show up in your recovery process. Finish this sentence: "[insert your name], I promise you that I will."

~~~~~

Connecting to a positive identity gives your life redefined and redirected meaning.

The PTSD lifestyle instills a very narrow vision of who you are. First and foremost, *"You are a trauma survivor."* It's like living in a big black canvas with only a tiny dot of white—if you're lucky.

Symptoms like intrusive thoughts, flashbacks, and nightmares keep your pain front and center while triggers, insomnia, and avoidant anxiety constantly remind you that you are living a *less-than* life. In the wake of these details, it's completely natural that you would develop an existence defined and directed by trauma, tragedy, low self-esteem, lack of confidence, guilt, shame and [*fill in your negative perceptions of yourself here*].

Is that the life you want?

Healing means overhauling your whole approach to life. Naturally, that extends to your perceptions of yourself, which is why creating and connecting to a more positive self-definition can be so beneficial in the recovery process. How you perceive who you are defines how you think, feel, and behave. If that person is someone "less than," undeserving, or worthless, it is much easier for traumatic memories and physiological responses to expand and take hold. Shifting into a state of energized, self-directed, execution-oriented activity, however, is the purpose of healing.

The ultimate intent of all trauma recovery is restoring you to a self and life that feels good, expresses your ideal and authentic self, engages your purpose, and allows you to become free of the negative effects of the past. This process includes restoring your social and professional functioning so that you are self-sufficient, self-trusting, and contributing to the world in meaningful ways. Now that's an identity to be proud of!

A positive post-trauma identity offers the successful realization of your desires and dreams. What are five qualities you'd like to embody in your recovered life? How can you practice having them now?

~~~~

In the future exists a you that is free, grounded, productive, and even joyful.

Okay, that may sound incredibly perky and optimistic and...that's just not what you need right now—or maybe it's *exactly* what you need!

It's easy to forget that you have choices and alternatives. It's easy to draw a blank when asked what your future looks like. The generalized healing thought here introduces the picture that waits for you to see, discover, and embody specific details.

Becoming that future person requires you to show up; be present; make peace with the past; shrug off the beliefs, fear, and blocks that hold you back; and dive into developing in the way that you would like to.

If you're thinking, "That's easier said than done," you're absolutely right. This isn't a book about *How to Easily Overcome PTSD*. This is a book about training your mind to focus in the right areas to support overcoming PTSD. There's only one way to do that: the hard way.

Do the hard thing: Let yourself hope for and imagine the healed, future you. What does that person look like? Close your eyes, imagine; write down what you see in your notebook, journal, or computer.

Note: *The first one hundred times you do this exercise, you may see absolutely nothing. In those times, gently invite (a piece of) the vision to appear. Continue practicing, and eventually it will fill in.*

~~~~

Joy is one of your innate qualities; if you give it a chance, it will naturally appear.

The experience of joyful pleasure is an inborn reflex, which means while the reflex may have been interrupted by trauma, you can reconnect the wires to begin experiencing the flow of a joyful current again. Like many healing tasks, tuning in to joy requires deliberate action on your part. You will have to go, see, do, try, and engage.

At first, the current will be small and you may not trust it, so it will be natural to suppress it or to accept just a little of the feeling. As you become accustomed to the idea of how deliberately you can connect to joy (plus your ability to handle it), the feeling of pleasure will grow, and you will become braver at reaching for it.

What simple experience brings you pleasure? It can be as normal as the feel of ice cream on your tongue or the sound of a breeze. Do one thing today that puts you in touch with the feeling of a healthy pleasure. Then schedule the creation of that feeling into every day for thirty consecutive days.

~~~~

Loving yourself helps you achieve safety and control.

When you hate yourself, you cause yourself to feel bad, worthless, undeserving, irresponsible, weak, powerless, insecure, incapable, isolated, disconnected, and alone. Whew, that's a powerful cocktail for putting yourself in danger!

On the other hand, loving yourself is the source of feeling connected, grounded, whole, secure, capable, powerful, and strong. The more you love yourself, the more you develop self-trust, compassion, empathy, adaptability, flexibility, and creativity. In other words, the more you love yourself, the more you develop strong survival skills that allow you to experience danger and act in self-protective ways. Loving yourself begins with saying, "I matter."

While it's a challenge, healing gains strength when you love part and eventually all of you, treating yourself with respect and compassion, and appreciating the job you've done in a situation that has been difficult.

Today, identify one part of you that is lovable, even in the smallest way. Practice sending some loving kindness to that self today: Close your eyes. Envision that self, and imagine sending a bright white loving light of energy out of your heart into hers, while at the same time saying, "You matter."

~~~~~

The greatest benefit of feeling joy is love—for yourself, the universe, and most importantly, for being alive.

There is much death in the post-trauma world: death of your past self and life; death of family or friends; death of inner connection; death of the imagined future; death of yourself, your soul, and who you wanted to be. Opening your pathways of joy opens the pathways for life.

One way to facilitate this process is to create your joy timelines.

Think back to your first pleasurable memory, and then work your way forward, looking for moments when you felt joy or delight (over even the simplest thing: the smell of a flower, the sight of the sunset). Whether you think forward from the beginning of your life or backward from today, what moments of delight reveal themselves to you?

Following the same procedure just described, identify what qualities you love about who you were or could have been at different ages throughout your life. At those times, that could have been your sense of curiosity or your love of baking. At other periods, it might have been the nurturing aspects of long daily bike rides or your willingness to take the risk of learning to jump off the high dive. As you look back over the years, list all of the qualities of your real self (or who you could have been) that make you feel a sense of you.

Based on the discoveries you made from the timelines, what did you previously enjoy (or wish you'd had a chance to enjoy) doing that you no longer do or experience? Plan to give yourself just a small taste of that again in the upcoming week.

Note: *Since your trauma, your interaction with pleasure will have become muted, and what brings you pleasure may have changed. In any joy exercise, be open both to old and new activities, engaging in them with an attitude of exploration until you find something that resonates with you.*

When you allow yourself to connect with and experience good things, you shrink down the effects, importance, and meaning of the bad things.

At first, engaging in any activity that feels good may feel bad, dangerous, or inappropriate. It may even seem ridiculous to make a priority out of feeling good, but you must! Feeling good is the light at the end of the tunnel. Allowing it to shine more brightly makes it easier to find your way.

Feel-good sensations are powerful catalysts for change and activate your engagement with your Core Self (or the you that could have been) that exists over the entire length of your lifetime. Connecting with that Core Self creates a sense of dependable safety as you link to a part of you that is strong, empowered, effective, and able to protect itself. This is the self you want to live from.

When you start feeling good, a fun thing will happen: You'll want to feel good more often. The reward center of your brain will start craving and looking for ways to activate more feel-good processes. There will be some healthy activity that starts to call your name, softly at first, then more insistently. Listen for the voice; notice the physical urge that accompanies it. Ply it with responses so that you spend more and more time engaging with your feeling-even-just-the-tiniest-bit-better self.

After so many months, or even years, of not allowing yourself, or being able, to feel pleasure, it can take a while for your

pleasure center to fully rev up. Daily pleasure engagement
(and in increasingly significant ways) encourages the process
to gain momentum naturally and at a pace you control.
What one healthy experience of pleasure can you create for
yourself today?

~~~~~

**You are more than scars and regrets and lost opportunities. You are
also future chances, undiscovered desires, and unexplored talents.**

With PTSD, the tendency is to see yourself and your life purely through
the lens of trauma. But that means you're seeing only a very small part of
the truth of who you are!

You are so much more than your trauma. When you lose this perspective
and allow only one phase of life to define who you are, you lose the richness
of your whole life itself.

Who you are and the value of the life you're living are measured over a
period of time. Your mission is to define who you are so that you can create
that value minute by minute.

Pause today and make a written list of things you value about
who you are. Think of things you've done in the past that you're
proud of; how you have helped others or yourself; moments
when you've taken an action that made a difference in the world,
even if that difference or the space in the world was small. Share
aspects of this list with someone you value: a close friend, a
family member, or even a pet. Invite them to make their own list
and share it with you.

~~~~~

Feed your good wolf today—the stronger she becomes, the sooner you will overcome PTSD.

Let this old Cherokee parable guide your intention today.

One evening, an old Cherokee man told his grandson about a battle that goes on inside people. He said: "My son, there is a battle between two wolves inside us all. One is Evil: It is anger, envy, jealousy, sorrow, regret, greed, arrogance, self-pity, guilt, resentment, inferiority, lies, false pride, superiority, and ego. The other is Good: It is joy, peace, love, hope, serenity, humility, kindness, benevolence, empathy, generosity, truth, compassion, and faith."

The grandson thought about it for a minute, and then asked his grandfather, "Which wolf wins?"

The old man simply replied: "The one you feed."

How can you feed your good wolf today?

Rise up and flow into your sense of powerfulness.

After trauma, your mind and body adapt to seeing the world in ways designed to keep you safe. This is true whether your trauma happened immediately following birth or after your first five, ten, or forty years of life. Your body, even if it is still wholly intact and unscarred, holds memories of what you experienced—whether that was physical in nature or not.

Throughout the day, your body and mind participate in an energetic exchange between themselves and the world around you; holding the negative energy of trauma affects them both and interferes with productive functioning, integration, and interaction with the outside world.

Moment by moment, however, the post-trauma world offers opportunities in which you can choose to give in to the feelings of powerlessness that your body and mind hold, or transcend them. Part of recovery is (re)learning that:

- You can trust yourself.
- The strength you used to survive still belongs to you.

- That strength can be accessed
  and applied in this moment.

When you live from an empowered "I can handle this!" place, the world changes from constant threat to neutral territory to a playground of opportunity.

How different would your world look if you approached every moment as if you would be successful? Imagine how this feeling would change how you live, love, work, feel, think, behave, and play. Identify one way you can implement this attitude today.

~~~~~

Decide you want to live arms-wide-open-to-the-sun.

It's perfectly natural for you to stop living after trauma, because time stopped at the point of your trauma. But you can't "live" in the place where time has stopped; you can only drift, space out, dissociate, and wait.

Healing requires that you crank up the clock; get it to tick again, and strongly. It means reconnecting to that desire to live, so that you get back into the world, living in a way that connects you to yourself, others, and the world in positive and meaningful ways.

Getting the machinery of wanting to live back into gear takes time. It requires a suspension of judgment, an openness to discovery, and an approach to reducing symptoms that goes beyond the boundaries of anxiety reduction out into the domain of love, fun, and joy. Odd concepts in the post-trauma world? It may seem like that at first, but they are, in fact, the concepts that can speed up your recovery in ways you never dared to hope.

Imagine that, in some alternate reality, there is a you living arms-wide-open-to-the-sun. How do you think that feels? What does that mean is true? What could you be doing that you're not doing today?

~~~~~~~

Ebb and flow are the nature of healing.

You've struggled for a long time. You want healing to come, so you commit to some sort of therapy, show up, go through the motions.

You believe recovery will happen just like that. And then you're shocked to feel a setback, or to not progress at the speed you (and others) expect.

The fact is, healing organically unfolds as a cumulative effort of conscious and subconscious methods involving your own personal ideas plus the guided objectives, inspirations, and actions of professionally trained trauma experts.

You are working hard to overcome post-traumatic stress symptoms; be kind to yourself. Celebrate your successes and remember these things:

1. Being hard on yourself only adds to the stress you already feel and slows down the healing process.

2. Perceived setbacks mean one thing and one thing only: You are human and still have more work to do.

Identify one thing you've done right in your recovery so far. (Can't think of something? How about: You accessed a moment of hope and picked up this book!) How can you celebrate that success?

Note: *Celebrations can be as small as giving yourself a hug, so give yourself a range in answering that question.*

~~~~~~~

Go out and play!

Regular life has so many have-tos, oughts, shoulds, and musts that it's easy to forget to include wishes, desires, and wants. Add in trauma, plus the heavy weight of the past, and it can become entirely foreign to even consider accessing a sense of frolic. But, if you neglect being playful and having fun, how can you ever fully (re)claim a joyful, calm, and peaceful life?

Really being alive comes from being driven by your life force. That is, the desire to live, experience, feel, see, touch, love, enjoy, discover, explore—and play. When you play, you access (or re-access) a sense of delight and whimsy—an unjaded part of yourself that doesn't think about the past or future; it thinks only about what it *likes* and *enjoys* in the present.

> When was the last time you thought about what you like and enjoy in the present? Challenge yourself to have at least five minutes of fun (anywhere on the scale of 1 to 10) today. What can you do to achieve that?

~~~~

The better you feel, the more you heal.

Key hormones that promote neuroplasticity include dopamine (your brain's chief pleasure neurotransmitter) and oxytocin (your brain's agent of trust and bonding). Because they are both natural mood enhancers, the scientific necessity of their presence in promoting change literally means that more healing can be achieved when you feel good versus bad. This is a key reason why connecting to a sense of joy (it's an inherent trait, so you are still capable of it regardless of how you feel today) can bring such deep benefits in recovery.

How you reconnect to a sense of joy will be as individual as your recovery process. Joy can be a sheer sense of ecstasy, or it can be the tiniest pleasure. When you begin implementing joy into your healing process, it will be important to define that joy in terms appropriate for who you are today. As with all other recovery tasks, reconnecting to joy can and should be something that you approach slowly and deliberately, with an attitude of exploration and discovery.

Up to now, you may have believed that happiness and joy will never be available to you again. That would be the equivalent of living during a drought and believing you will never again see rain. Nature works in cycles. Droughts always end; so will yours. Even the smallest success in this area can have the effect of turning on a light in the darkness of your mind.

Joy's number one benefit comes from its life-affirming properties. What activity or experience makes you feel that it's good to be alive? This can be anything from attending an outdoor concert to bodysurfing through some waves. How can you give yourself this experience?

Note: Expecting yourself to be ready to engage in all-out joy at this point in your healing process may be unreasonable. If that's the case, focus on giving yourself a comfortable experience that brings you the genuine feeling of neutrality (versus depressed despair) or slight happiness. What might offer you that experience today? Try it.

PART TWO

THE FACTS YOU NEED TODAY

English Renaissance philosopher Francis Bacon said, "Knowledge is power." In PTSD recovery, it is also the key to *reclaiming your power*. The more you know and understand how trauma affects your brain and the science behind your symptoms, the more you will appreciate important things, including:

- There are neurophysiological processes occurring beyond your control.

- You are separate from your symptomatic behaviors.

- There are ways to reverse the effects of trauma.

- Your brain contains key components for change that encourage healing.

With this knowledge, you can identify your personal issues, clarify an approach to resolving them, and implement a process to address the recovery you desire. Education in the PTSD world is priceless. In this section, you will discover key points that can lead to *Aha!* moments that change both how you see yourself and, if you share them, how others see you.

YOU ARE HAVING A NORMAL REACTION TO AN ABNORMAL EXPERIENCE

You are entitled to your post-trauma response. You are also entitled to heal.

Since your trauma, you may notice that your mind and body operate and function differently than they used to. The changes you've observed are real and valid. Your mind and body have not yet found a way to effectively recalibrate. This happens to many people. Some of your post-trauma symptoms come from deeply instinctive reactions below consciousness. Others derive from thoughts (based on new post-trauma beliefs) that activate physical responses and emotional reactions.

Viktor Frankl, a Holocaust survivor and the father of logotherapy, said, "An abnormal reaction to an abnormal experience is normal behavior." Although symptoms may make you feel crazy, your response to trauma originates in a sane space: the desire to feel safe and in control. While others around you may not understand or experience the same post-trauma response, your response is normal for you. It makes sense given who you are, what your history has been, and how your brain and body operate.

When you feel the effects of amplified symptoms, remind yourself: "This aroused, survival-oriented self is separate from the whole Me that I am."

~~~~~~~

The word *trauma* descends from the Greek word for wound.

If you feel as though you've experienced a wound to your mind, body, or soul, you're not alone. Research suggests that up to 70 percent of all US adults will experience a trauma in their lifetime; up to 20 percent of those will go on to develop post-traumatic stress disorder.

While the media highlights combat veterans and we all know that car accidents can be traumatizing, as a society, we don't often define what trauma is or even talk about what causes it, which can leave you thinking that your experience wasn't "bad enough" to qualify as traumatic. You don't have to qualify your experience or judge it against that of someone else. Trauma is trauma and includes:

- any experience that is less than nurturing

- feeling emotionally overwhelmed

- an event that overwhelms your ability to cope

- physically feeling out of control

- an event that causes the feeling of powerlessness

- dissociation and/ or detachment

- a change in how you see your place in the world

- a disturbing situation

- fear for physical or emotional well-being and safety

- incidents of interpersonal aggression

- chronic abusive situations (physical, verbal, emotional)

- an emotional shock that creates lasting psychological damage

- recurring distressing events

- a serious injury to the body

You have experienced trauma, which means you have personal insights into what it means to be traumatized. In your notebook, journal, or computer, add your definition to the preceding list.

~~~~~

The more you know and understand about PTSD and how it affects you, the safer and more effective you will be in healing.

Elements of shame, fear, anger, guilt, and grief often get in the way of a calm, focused understanding of PTSD and how it alters you. The following list offers an overview of ten major things to understand about yourself while dealing with symptoms of PTSD:

1. **Knowledge is power.** Understanding the process of a triggering event, the psychic reaction to trauma, the warning signs and symptoms of PTSD, and available treatment options for PTSD helps you recognize, support, and guide yourself toward diagnosis, treatment, and healing.

2. **Trauma changes you.** After trauma, you want to believe that life can return to the way it was, that you can continue as who you were. This is not how it works. Trauma leaves a huge and indelible impact on the soul. It is impossible to endure trauma and not experience some type of psychic shift.

3. **PTSD hijacks your identity.** One of the biggest problems with PTSD is that it takes over your entire view of yourself, so that you no longer see yourself clearly. Rather than seeing the Real You (your powerful core, authentic self), you know, see, and experience life only from your powerless Survivor Self.

4. **Your life force is out of balance.** In response to trauma, the Real You retreated, and your Survivor Self emerged to keep you safe. While both are powerful origins of your will to live, the Real You alone contains elements that create a life that feels good when you're living it. Rebalancing your life force by allowing the Real You to resume control is the path to addressing the ultimate damage that recovery must repair.

5. **Often, you cannot help how you behave.** There are two reasons for this. (1) You are operating on a sort of autopilot; you are not always in control. (2) Trauma affects your neurobiology; symptoms occur because of your overactive sympathetic nervous system. PTSD is an

exaggerated state of survival mode in which your executive brain (which inhibits unwanted behaviors) often shuts down.

6. **You cannot always be logical.** Since your perspective is driven by fear, you don't always think straight, nor do you always accept the advice of those who do. This is grounded in the science of how trauma affects the brain and is amplified by PTSD-driven emotions.

7. **You cannot just "get over it."** From the outside, it's easy to imagine that a certain amount of time passes, memories fade, and trauma gets relegated to the history of a life. Unfortunately, with untended PTSD, nothing fades. Neither your body nor your mind lets you forget. Because of altered neurobiological processes that leave memories unconsolidated and survival mechanisms activated, you cannot blithely walk away from the past without the support of significant healing practices.

8. **You are not in denial—you're coping!** Living with PTSD takes a tremendous effort. Even if you don't admit it, you know there's something wrong. Sometimes, the biggest step you make toward recovery is simply getting up and continuing your daily routine.

9. **You do not hate everyone.** Contrary to the ways you might behave, somewhere inside, you do know that others are often not the source of your problems, even while you blame them.

10. **The presence of others matters.** PTSD creates a great sense of isolation. In your post-traumatic state, it makes a difference to know that there are people who will stand by you.

Who do you know who would benefit from seeing this list? Educate others about PTSD and own these concepts by sharing this list with someone else.

Knowing things in your mind that you don't feel in your body is a typical disconnect in trauma recovery.

For example, think of some disturbing aspect of your trauma and say out loud, "That happened in the past." You know it's a fact, but how much does your body feel the truth?

When you struggle with the aftereffects of trauma, there's always an instant when you become aware that, cognitively, you know the event(s) is (are) over. Yet you are very aware that, in your body, either you feel nothing or still experience frequent, unexpected, and unwanted overreactive responses to new situations that trigger old fears.

One way to begin healing the disconnect is to use the following practice.

Identify any random statement that your mind knows and enter it in your notebook, journal, or computer. (Use a non-triggering statement like "The sky is blue.")

Match up that statement with the equivalent feeling in your body. Where in your body do you feel that?

Then write down your answers to the following questions:

- How does your body feel the truth of what your mind knows?

- How does it create that feeling?

- What color, size, and shape is that feeling?

Your body and mind are actually very good at syncing up. Try the preceding practice again using a slightly more sensitive statement. Notice how your body creates the equivalent feeling. Continue increasing the sensitivity of the statement until you get to the one that you usually can't feel; see what comes up. Repeat several times to allow the feeling to gently connect and reveal itself.

Note: *Different ideas and experiences may be represented in different places in your body.*

Your mind has good reasons for what it does in the PTSD state.

The first thing most PTSD survivors do is hate themselves, their symptoms, and their irrational, unstoppable behaviors. Take a time-out from that and appreciate that your mind and body are doing the one thing your subconscious mind most values: finding a way to keep you safe.

The problem in PTSD is that the complex psychological and neurobiological systems of your mind and body haven't received the message that the danger has passed. Since they still believe that imminent danger exists, they are doing exactly the right things to ensure your survival.

While these behaviors do not always make your life easier, they do have a purpose. Like any good detective, you have to figure out the clues your mind offers up—and then direct it to take healthy actions based on what it seems to need.

> What do you need most today: a sense of safety or a feeling of control? How can you answer that need with a smart choice and strong action that are grounded in healthy, self-supportive elements?

Ninety-eight percent of what you do every day is habit.

Every morning you wake up and get out of bed in a fluid motion. You don't lie there thinking: First, I have to sit up and then swing my legs over the side of the bed and place my feet on the floor.

You've successfully moved through this process over a thousand times before; you know how it goes and do it without thinking of the individual steps. The reason you do this is that your brain creates patterns based on repetitive practices, so that you develop a shorthand. You think, "Get out of bed," and the process activates.

The same is true for all of your PTSD habits. Once they were fresh; now they are ingrained practices housed in neural pathways designed to help you do things ever more efficiently and expertly.

The question is: How many of these habits are good for you?

For the next twenty-four hours, notice your PTSD-driven habits, the ones based in anxiety, hypervigilance, hyperarousal, and fear. It's time to begin the process of dismantling them (slowly) and replacing them with others that sustain and feed your energy, rather than deplete it.

Which PTSD habit do you feel ready to break? What's one step you can take in that direction?

Being in control is a major PTSD and trauma coping mechanism. Learning to release control is a major recovery—healing—process.

Trauma represents a moment (or more) when you were disastrously without control. The survival response that got put in place afterward drives you to do just about anything to be in control again.

However, a frantic quality comes with trying to control everything about every moment you're in. If things are under control one minute, you have to worry about what's coming next. All of this leads to increased anxiety, which feeds on itself until you're a hamster on the PTSD wheel.

The outcome? You try harder to be in control, which leads to larger experiences proving you're not in control, which leads to increased symptoms and a spiral spinning...you got it: further out of control!

The more you try to be in control, the more out of control you will feel. Being aware that the quest for control begets *less* control is the beginning of truly being more *in* control.

Shifting your focus from external control to internal self-connection results in healthier self-protection strategies. This way of thinking reduces your brain's threat-scan activity and ultimately makes you more adaptable, flexible, and creative, the true hallmarks of being in control.

In what area of life do you spend the most energy attempting to be in control? If you were to do that a little less, what would have to happen?

~~~~~

PTSD and constriction go hand in hand.

In her landmark book *Trauma and Recovery*, Judith Herman defines constriction as "the numbing response of surrender." It is, actually, a very reasonable response to trauma. At a time when you feel vulnerable, it makes perfect sense to lessen that vulnerability by turning your life into something small, airtight, comfortable, and most of all, controlled by you.

However, feeling safe and in control can come from negative or positive actions. Becoming agoraphobic, for example, offers terrific control but limits the possibilities for who you are and how you live.

Finding healthy ways to feel safe helps restore your feeling of self-efficacy (personal power) while offering you healthy control in a lifestyle that allows you to grow, live, and succeed in moving past your past. The objective in recovery is to replace the negative, constriction-oriented behaviors with positive options, choices, and actions.

Everything in PTSD recovery is about taking small steps to get to the big successes. If constriction is a normal response to symptoms of post-traumatic stress, then healing means releasing the restrictions—in a slow, safe way. Consider all the ways that you constrict yourself and your life. What one area do you feel willing to explore being a little less constricting in? What can you do to test loosening your control there?

~~~~~

Beliefs are at the core of every choice you make and every action you take.

Without your being consciously aware of them, beliefs play an enormous role in how you live, love, work, play, and experience what it is to be you. They do this by influencing how you perceive, understand, order, and predict stimuli, information, and experience.

Depending on your beliefs, you will feel motivated, committed to heal, and capable of evolving toward your Future Self—or trapped, stuck, and destined to live a life full of symptoms. After trauma, beliefs can function to open you to experiences or shut down your ability to experience at all.

Part One: Become very conscious of your post-trauma beliefs. Since your trauma occurred, what do you believe is true about yourself, others, and the world? Write out ten beliefs for each area. How, if at all, do they affect your recovery?

Part Two: This week, set up a habit of checking in with your beliefs at random moments. Ask, "What do I believe is true in this moment?" Then assess—is this a belief that supports who you wish to be? If it isn't, you've just hit on an area that requires your attention to transform. Identify the belief you'd rather hold, and take steps to live it. (See page 101 and explore the thought, "Your beliefs drive 100 percent of your behavior" to begin more in-depth belief transformation.)

~~~~~

How you perceive and think about something creates your experience of it.

Events and circumstances are purely objective. That is, they happen and are neither good nor bad; they just *are*.

The interpretation and meaning you give to them create how you feel about them. Everything is put through your *subjective* filter.

Here's the good news: You control that filter, which means you control how you see something and the feeling that perception creates.

> This will sound like a concept too simple to apply in a very complex PTSD world, but it works to train your brain:
>
> If you want to feel something different, then you must find a more comfortable, supportive, and positively proactive point of view, one thought at a time. In uncomfortable moments, test this process over the next couple of days by asking yourself, "What's another way to look at this that would feel just a little bit better?"

~~~~~~

The place where a fracture heals is stronger than the rest of the bone.

Some people (including trauma professionals) say that survivors with PTSD are like a bone that's broken: The fracture will eventually knit and heal, but it will always be weak, undependable, and prone to more breaks in the same place.

The next time someone offers you this erroneous analogy, share this scientific fact:

Bones are *stronger* in the places where they reknit. After you heal, you are stronger than you were before.

Hold on to this idea, too: As healed bones can be more sensitive to temperature and weather change, you too can become more sensitive and intuitively connected with yourself and the world.

Consider these questions:

- What if you yourself are like a bone healing after a break?
- What if, in the place where you have been fractured, your soul heals and becomes even stronger?

- What if your healed breaks strengthen your intuition, which, as Gavin de Becker suggests in *The Gift of Fear*, is already one of your innate assets?

Spend some time today being open to the idea that, as you travel this healing journey, you are actually becoming a better, stronger, and safer version of yourself. How does that knowledge change your perspective?

THE SCIENCE BEHIND YOUR SYMPTOMS...AND RECOVERY

The reactions you feel in any moment (fear, anger, love, etc.) are manifestations of your neurobiology.

That is, the biology of your nervous system and how it responds to internal and external cues. The key player in that scenario is your brain.

The most significant concept to embrace is that your brain's structure changes in response to experience. Literally, your brain develops new neural pathways as it encodes every experience you have. Your brain's willingness to change is why trauma can have such devastating effects; your brain took in the experience and changed.

Yet your brain's willingness to change for the worse is also why it's eminently possible for you to feel better: New experiences can and will change your brain again.

Interrupting the patterns that trauma put into place is not just a process done in the mind or accomplished in the body; it is achieved in both, through a program that integrates science and psychology.

Think about the traumatic experience(s) that caused your brain to change. What fears motivated those changes? What new experience would introduce your brain to an opposite (safety-stimulating) event?

~~~

Trauma affects your brain function.

Understanding how trauma changes your brain can pack tremendous power into your process. For one thing, it takes the blame off you. There's science behind your symptoms.

Here are some important facts to know:

1. Your brain has three levels, each related to different types and areas of functioning:

   • *Reptilian (deep inner brain):* responsible for your instincts and automatic body processing

   • *Mammalian (midbrain):* responsible for emotional processing and sensory relay

   • *Neomammalian (outer brain):* responsible for cognitive processing and decision-making

Trauma affects each level and causes dysregulation in your overall functioning that creates the symptoms you experience every day. In survival mode, your reptilian brain takes over, knocking offline the neomammalian structures that usually inhibit survival-oriented behaviors.

2. Many structures in your brain engage during a traumatic moment, but four important ones play critical roles when you're in survival mode:

   • brain stem   • hippocampus

   • amygdala   • prefrontal cortex

How these four structures interact and function individually affects how you feel during and after trauma. When they over- or under-function, they change how you think, process information, sleep, and even behave.

3. Your body and mind are designed to fluctuate between response and repair. Due to the increase or decrease in several chemicals that send messages to different systems, your body knows to gear up to fight/flee/freeze or rest and restore.

After trauma, however, some of these chemicals can remain high, such as the stress hormone cortisol. When this powerful stress responder is pegged at the high end of its range, it causes far-reaching effects on your brain, including the inability to lay down a new memory or even access an old one. The presence of cortisol lessens how effectively brain cells communicate with each other by interfering with the function of neurotransmitters (how those cells send messages).

4. Research has shown three fascinating findings about how your brain changes—again and again, for worse and then better—in relation to trauma:

- When your amygdala overreacts to trauma (constantly signaling threat and danger), it can actually increase in size.

- When your hippocampus underreacts to trauma (stops fully processing and storing memories), it can actually decrease in size.

- With treatment, both of these changes can often be reversed: The amygdala can shrink back to, and the hippocampus can regain, normal size.

> How does this information change what you understand about yourself? Place a marker on this page; the next time you're disturbed by symptoms, return here and remind yourself that the origins of symptoms stem from brain changes.

～～～

You cannot "just get over it."

The more you understand that brain change (including chemistry, biology, and neurophysiology) plays a role in the symptoms you experience, the more you will recognize that trauma isn't something you're holding on to; it's something that has a hold on you.

Memorize these facts:

- **PTSD is science, not choice.** The presence of post-trauma symptoms indicates changes in the brain caused by trauma. This happens automatically from the way that trauma is experienced by both your mind and body.

- **Amygdala becomes sensitized.** Part of your primal, instinctual brain, the amygdala is responsible for detecting threat and danger. When it becomes highly sensitized due to a traumatic experience, it can constantly see threat everywhere, which means it keeps you in an elevated state of anxiety, hyperarousal, hypervigilance, and a fear frame of mind.

- **Hippocampus is hijacked.** Located adjacent to the amygdala, the hippocampus is responsible for consolidating memories and shifting them out of short-term and into long-term status. Trauma can interrupt and disable normal hippocampal functioning so that memories are not properly consolidated, which means you can be overwhelmed by intrusive thoughts, flashbacks, and the feeling that the trauma is still very present.

- **Brain stem overflows with sensory stimulation.** Part of your reptilian brain and located at the back of your brain, your brain stem collects sensory information from your body and feeds it into the brain. If you're in a hyper-aroused state, the majority of this information will amplify those feelings via sensory details.

- **Prefrontal cortex becomes overwhelmed by sensory stimulation.** Located in the front of your brain (right behind your forehead), the prefrontal cortex is the seat of your executive function. For example, it helps you think rationally, plus make decisions and take actions. It's also in charge of inhibiting the activity of your lower brain levels. A normally functioning brain properly filters incoming sensory information according to what's relevant; nonoptimal functioning allows in an overflow of input, which means your brain gets too much information that it can't prioritize and then shuts down in response to the sense of feeling overwhelmed, leaving your lower and more primal brain structures running the show.

When others tell you to "let it go already" or "just get over it," hear them really saying, "I don't know enough about how PTSD affects you to appreciate what you're going through." The next time someone (including the voice in your head) tells you to "let it go," reply by sharing this information.

~~~~~

Brain changes caused by PTSD impair your ability to direct and maintain your attention.

Attention is an inhibitory function that tells the brain and other systems to resist being distracted and remain focused in one area. Built from many individual processes, there are two main sources:

- **Posterior brain (bottom):** This is your noncognitive, early aspect of attention that automatically occurs from sensory input. Specifically, this relates to your vision (processed from the first hundredth of a millisecond of perceived stimuli) and spatial orienting (processed through both your eyes and ears, sending information and causing your attention to shift to the originating source). Because noticing these types of stimuli is noncognitive, you have *zero control* over how, when, where, and in what way you do notice. Impairment of this area (in ways that cause it to be overactive) can contribute to sleep disruption, sensory overload, confusion, and a feeling of dullness.

- **Prefrontal Cortex (top):** This is your entirely cognitive, late aspect of attention that determines meaning and action. Choosing what is salient, this process occurs one to three seconds after the stimulus is perceived. Dysregulation of this area can cause symptoms including hypervigilance, hyperarousal, depression, fear, anxiety, panic, impulsivity, hyperactivity, rage, and irritability. Likewise, an underactive prefrontal cortex and overactive posterior cortex can produce hypervigilance and hyperarousal. Ideally, the left side of your prefrontal cortex (responsible for speech and the seat of your approach-oriented, joyful brain) should be more active than the right. After trauma, however, the left side often dials down, and the right prefrontal cortex (your sorrow center) plays more of a role. The imbalance of right over left can lead to less facility for language, plus contribute to your experiencing more anger, irritability, withdrawal, rage, and constant perceived threat.

To make matters even more complex—and contribute to symptoms like nightmares, intrusive thoughts, and flashbacks—another part of the brain, the anterior cingulate, can also stop functioning optimally. An upside-down Nike swoosh located just above your corpus callosum (a broad band of nerve fibers connecting your brain's two hemispheres) on either side of your brain, your anterior cingulate is a big, fat string of tissue responsible for helping you switch your attention from one object to another. It also helps determine relevance or the importance of something attracting your attention. After trauma, and particularly in PTSD, the anterior cingulate can become locked in a cycle. Instead of switching attention, it remains focused on one object, ruminating without cease.

You can reclaim control over your attention by consciously shifting it. The next time you notice intrusive thoughts, pause, take a step back, and say, "That's just my brain becoming locked in a cycle again."

Then consciously redirect your attention by engaging in a distracting experience for five to thirty minutes. While doing this, engage as many of your senses as possible: consciously see, feel, hear, taste, and smell what you are doing.

Obsessive or compulsive behavior is a natural element of the PTSD brain.

The purpose of the attention process is to both notice and tune out. In a perfectly working system, you briefly recognize stimuli and then move on, returning your attention to a chosen place of importance.

For attention to work properly, the bottom and top processes need to balance so that you decide how, when, and where to direct your attention. In PTSD, this process becomes dysregulated:

- Your hypersensitive amygdala notices more threat than actually exists; in misfiring an enormous number of times, it creates an attention bias for both noticing threat and constantly scanning for stimuli.

- Your automatic (bottom) orienting attention pulls your cognitive (top) attention off other things because it frequently determines that threat is present and needs to be noticed.

- The resulting state of flooding from the sensory system inhibits your prefrontal cortex; the influx of information becomes so overwhelming that the cortex cannot maintain its ability to focus attention.

- In an environment so filled with sensory cues, it becomes impossible for your cortex to be selective, an action that would inhibit the amygdala's overactive behavior.

- Dysregulation results in a habit of preferentially scanning for arousal that impairs the balanced process of receiving and processing stimuli.

In this state, the shift from reactive to responsive mode fails to activate or complete; your default mode becomes threat management, a situation that depletes brain resources and leads to a mind that can neither quiet itself nor appropriately shift its attention or inhibit actions. This results in obsessive and compulsive behavior.

What behavior or behaviors have you developed that are obsessive or compulsive? The next time it occurs, pause for a moment to notice and to inspect it from the standpoint of arousal: What threat is this behavior trying to ameliorate? How real is the threat? How (else) can it be resolved? Intentionally shift your attention from the obsessive behavior to a healthier response.

~~~~

Every thought you have sends electrical impulses and releases chemicals that produce sensations (feelings) in your body.

Scientifically speaking, a thought produces a physical reaction. You may not always be aware of the thought before the feeling; many thoughts can fly below the radar of your consciousness. When this happens and you notice a disturbing feeling, try this:

- Become very mindful of your surroundings and what you've experienced in the past five minutes.

- Check your senses (what have you heard, seen, felt, smelled, or tasted?).

- Revisit your interactions (with others, a chore, a project).

- Look for a disturbing association (i.e., a person who looks untrustworthy or a sound that reminds you of your trauma).

- Listen to the voice inside your head; what is it saying?

Doing this kind of work can uncover the unnoticed thought that led to the feeling, which can clue you in to a new area of focus in your healing process. When you feel a sense of discomfort, test this process today.

~~~

Your brain changed due to trauma; in every moment it contains the possibility to change again.

In his book *The Brain That Changes Itself*, about how willing and hardwired your brain is for change, Dr. Norman Doidge writes, "We can change our brain anatomy simply by using our imagination." The proof of this statement lies in many hard-core scientific experiments. In other words, it's irrefutable: You are a being designed to change over and over and over, and that process can happen simply by activating neuroplastic changes through *imagination*.

If you accept this as truth (which it is), then you also have to accept that one of the most compelling and effective tools in creating brain change is... your own choices and actions for how you use your brain.

Yes, trauma changed your brain, but today it is poised, ready, and willing to change again.

A pure, untraumatized, authentic self exists despite your experiences; it is the part that wishes to be whole and free.

Practice imagining that self, plus what it can, will, and is ready to do to help you heal.

~~~

A more functional brain leads to more successful recovery work.

The way trauma affects your brain has large consequences for how your life moves forward. Healing symptoms ranging from anxiety to sleep and mood disturbances, memory loss, concentration challenges, and emotional dysregulation are often possible—even more probable—when you give your brain what it needs to function at an optimal level.

There are five major areas you control that affect how your brain functions. Choosing to flex your muscle in these areas can seriously increase the level at which your brain works:

- **Cognitive function depends on food.** Your brain consumes a huge amount of energy in relation to the rest of your body. The successful process of transferring energy from food to your neurons (which make synapses that send signals throughout your brain and body) is critical to allowing your brain to function optimally. This means making healthy food choices.

- **Neurogenesis promotes processing.** "Neurogenesis" is the birth of new neurons in the brain. Old belief: By adolescence, your brain has a set number of neurons. New scientific fact: Fresh neurons can be grown throughout your lifetime. More and healthier neurons respond to stimuli, communicate, and conduct impulses even more efficiently. You can stimulate neurogenesis by engaging your brain in (1) learning, (2) the element of surprise, and (3) activities of significant importance.

- **Brain processes strengthen through your ability to focus.** Doing recovery work means you have to focus on specific ideas, tasks, and processes. This can be tough to do when your brain just flat-out refuses to concentrate. Developing your strength in this area is a major step in reclaiming your power to affect the healing you desire. Practice brain training and focus exercises, e.g., solitaire, concentration, puzzles, and both off- and online brain-training programs and video games.

- **Emotional processes strengthen through your ability to tolerate.** Healing from trauma often involves facing fears, uncomfortable memories, and disturbing thoughts. It is tough to be present in a state that induces feelings of anxiety, panic, and the urge to fight, flee, or freeze. Relieving symptoms, however, happens when you become stronger than they are. Learning to expand yourself so that you tolerate emotions is critical in this process.

- **Optimal physical conditions change your brain.** When your brain is in survival mode and your sympathetic nervous system is charged up, it's hard to think, make rational decisions, or engage in analytical thought processes. To really work the way you need (and want) it to, your brain needs an internal environment to support clarity, logic, flexibility, and creative patterns. Ways to train your brain for this include breathwork, meditation, and mindfulness.

Make full use of this information (and develop a plan for putting it into action) by listening to the free "Reversing How Trauma Affects Your Brain" webinar series on ChangeYouChoose.com/webinar-archives.

Scientifically speaking, caffeine makes you more likely to feel fear, anger, and anxiety while chemically preventing your ability to feel safe, calm, and happy.

If you've ever lost a night's sleep due to post-trauma issues, then you know what it's like to carry both the emotional baggage and physical deprivation of feeling as though you've been hit by a Mack truck overnight. It's natural to reach for energy boosters, but here's the problem: managing with sugar and caffeine—especially caffeine—creates bigger problems for trauma survivors stuck in the trauma loop.

Here's why: When you're awake, the chemical adenosine slowly accumulates in your brain and binds to specific adenosine receptors. The result: Your brain activity slows down. The more adenosine your brain acquires, the more tired you feel. On the other hand, while you sleep, adenosine decreases in your brain, which allows you to wake up feeling refreshed. The caffeine in coffee is very similar to adenosine in structure.

Once ingested, caffeine moves through your bloodstream to your brain, where it competes with adenosine for the receptors. Ultimately, caffeine muscles out the adenosine so that it can't bind; the calming properties of adenosine are eliminated. This may be great for a short burst of energy; however, with long-term caffeine infusions, your brain responds by creating more receptors, which causes you to need more caffeine to reach the same energized feeling. This is why, if you miss your caffeine fix or decide to quit, you'll experience withdrawal symptoms and feel even more tired than you would have originally.

Another way caffeine increases your feelings of energy is by stimulating the production of adrenaline—your fight-or-flight hormone. (You know, the very aspect of post-trauma living you're trying to avoid!) The outcome is to increase your heart rate and circulation, plus open up your airways. Adrenaline also affects dopamine levels (the hormone that makes you happy) by *preventing* its reabsorption in the brain. In one fell swoop, your brain goes from having the capacity to feel better to not.

So, how's a survivor supposed to cope without energy? Try these caffeine-free, energy-increasing alternatives:

- Make a green smoothie.
- Drink water with lemon zest.
- Brew some licorice tea.
- Sip some pomegranate juice.
- Down some wheatgrass juice.
- Make a cup of schizandra tea.
- Stock up on carob powder.

~~~~~~

You and your brain change through the repetition of experience.

Scientists call it "spaced practice" when you repeat an exercise consistently over time; this builds new neural pathways. They call it "massed practice" when you repeat a new skill several times in a short period of time. This behavior also builds and solidifies new neural pathways. To summarize, the more you do something, the more your brain learns how to do it more quickly and efficiently.

Engaging in any activity provides an experience to which your brain responds. This response leads to the release of chemicals that can elevate or sink your mood. The PTSD lifestyle already offers plenty of opportunities to practice feeling bad. Healing deeply benefits from feeling good.

If you want to change, you need to give yourself enough practice at feeling good that your brain has a chance to build neural pathways for it.

How do you do that? Try practicing a little mindfulness...

Check in with yourself throughout the day. Notice when you feel less bad, neutral, or on the positive side of good. This can be a relatively calm moment in the presence of a friend or feeling grateful for the smell of warm, clean laundry. Let yourself hang out in these small moments of mindfulness for at least thirty seconds.

Note: *The more you experience moments connecting to a sense of your own effective proficiency, the more naturally those skills (and the feelings they create) will be available to you in moments of both low and high stress.*

~~~~~~~

It is entirely possible for your brain to change (for the better) during PTSD recovery.

Neuropsychologist Dr. Rick Hanson explains: "The brain takes its shape from whatever it rests upon." What he means is that brain structure constantly changes as a result of the information flowing through it. Indulge your negativity bias (focus on the bad things), and your brain's activity and development will reinforce all of the feelings and neuronal structures that support that.

Or develop your positivity bias (your ability to be optimistic, for example), and you can develop a wholly different set of neural pathways (and often reverse the damage created by trauma) that create a very healthy, whole, and healing brain.

Bringing yourself out of survival mode and into life mode requires many changes, and lots of diligent work, perseverance, guidance, and support. Along the way, there are practices you can develop that help train your brain to make the changes you desire. Giving your brain experiences that promote the ideas, beliefs, sensations, and feelings you wish to have offers it a process for creating and recreating them over and over.

Begin developing a healthy sense of safety by implementing daily healthy safety practices that allow you to create and notice a sense of well-being.

Add to this process by holding that sensation of safety for thirty seconds multiple times a day. This exercise develops new neural pathways that become new habits that can help reduce stress and triggers and increase your calm, confidence, and control—all of which adds up to effective progress in healing PTSD.

> Identify a person, place, thing, or action that makes you feel safe. Plan to connect with an experience of this as often as possible for thirty consecutive days.

Help your brain change.

In 1904, neuroanatomist Ramón y Cajal argued that thoughts, repeated in "mental practice," strengthen existing neuronal connections and create new ones. This is the foundation of why imagination (and using your imagination daily to see in your mind what you want in your life) can be so productive in recovery.

Just running a little movie in your head once or twice a day for a few minutes can actually start to change the structure of your brain. It's free; it's easy; it's effective.

> Add this to your daily schedule (two to three times a day):
>
> - Choose a safe and quiet space in which you will be uninterrupted.
>
> - Place your body in a comfortable position.
>
> - Identify one significant change you'd like to see in your behavior.
>
> - If it feels comfortable, close your eyes.
>
> - Take a deep breath in and slowly exhale.

- Imagine there's a movie screen in your mind; see an image of yourself on the screen in the moment *just before* a situation that requires the wanted behavior.

- Let the movie begin to play forward; watch yourself do the behavior you desire.

- When the movie ends, let it start over; watch through fully four times.

- On the fifth run-through, imagine you can step into the image of yourself on the screen; notice what it feels like to be in this body and see through these eyes.

- Let the movie play forward again; deeply experience what it feels like to consciously engage in the wanted behavior. (Repeat at least three times or as many times as you desire.)

- Spend a moment savoring the feeling of accomplishment.

- When you're ready, bring your awareness back to your present environment and open your eyes.

~~~~~

The potential for you to experience forward motion, relief, and even freedom exists in every moment, neuronal connection, and synapse into which you breathe.

In the presence of PTSD symptoms, your brain structures become sensitized to pain, fear, anxiety, panic, terror, etc. Since your brain changes in response to experience in the recovery process, it can be very helpful to deliberately create and connect to joyful, fun, taking-in-the-good experiences. (At first you might resist, but that's okay!)

You are, already, more in control than you realize: From imagination to attention training to having positive experiences, there are ways you can support brain change every day. Starting today, you can sensitize your brain to pleasure, delight, happiness, contentment, and gratitude. The major key to doing this? Creating experiences that allow your mind to have a positive experience and combining them with mindful awareness practices that allow you to hold onto the feeling of that good experience for at least twenty to thirty seconds.

Two options for testing this practice today:

- Think back over your past—very recent or very distant: What activity (regardless of how fleeting or small) have you ever done that made you feel happy to be alive, free, strong, excited, joyful, or have a sense of pleasure? (Resist the temptation to respond that there's never been such a moment; there has.) Create a way to experience that sensation again and again, as often as possible.

- Or follow these steps three to six times a day:

  1. Choose an activity that brings you a sense of pleasure (Resist the impulse to judge how much pleasure)

  2. Engage in this activity slower than you ever have before and really be aware of what it feels like.

  3. Focus on that good feeling for a solid twenty to thirty seconds.

~~~~~~

You need to restore as often as you react.

Your nervous system automatically shifts from reactive mode (energy-expending) to responsive mode (energy-restoring). In survival mode, your body amps up heart rate, breathing, and stress hormones. Afterward, your body has an instinctual process for shifting into responsive mode, which reduces all of those elements when the survival response is no longer necessary.

Because trauma and the lack of its resolution interrupt the biological processes required for the reactive/responsive shift, it's easy to understand how that activity can be derailed, plus the effect that has on both the body and the mind. With high stress hormones and your sympathetic nervous system always in reactive mode, your body systems (e.g., digestion, reproduction) will be affected, which results in aberrant alterations in their functioning.

What if that same kind of process applies to the mind too? Like your body, all nonessential mind processes become suspended during trauma. They include a connection to intuition, thought and feeling awareness, desire, and choice-making. In psychological survival mode, all that matters is detecting threats and being prepared for danger. These are autonomic processes that overwhelm and disconnect your inner connection processes, narrowing those activities so that, instead of having a full range of emotions and thoughts to experience, you have only those attuned to trauma and its associations.

While there's no scientific theory outlining a psychological downshift that parallels your body's natural stress reduction process, you can imagine that your mind itself needs to go through a similar reactive/responsive transition. Put in place or deepen a daily practice of mindfulness, meditation, breathwork, yoga, or other such program that offers both your body and your mind opportunities to restore.

~~~~~

Train yourself to be more present, more versatile, and less serious.

Life-force living means experiencing yourself and the world from a perspective of being happy to be alive. Life-force thinking challenges you to throw off the chains of trauma thoughts and free yourself into the buoyant ocean of feeling good. By cultivating a sense of play in both small and large daily and individual moments, you can transform your personal trauma psychology from intrusive and redundant thinking to open, fresh, and new choices and actions.

Not digging this idea? Do it for science: The happier your brain is, the more plastic and changeable it becomes. Consider these scientific facts about the benefits of play and how it affects the way you think:

- releases endorphins that elevate mood

- leads to a sense of connection and community

- develops trust, adaptability, and learning

- improves memory

- stimulates the growth of the cerebral cortex (the seat of your executive function)

- promotes problem-solving

Keep a log of how you put a sense of play into every day. Open yourself to being surprised at where a playful, fun feeling can come from...and how small the origin of it can be.

PART THREE

STRENGTHEN YOUR RECOVERY PROCESS

There are varying levels of engagement in the PTSD recovery mission:

- **Level One:** Acknowledging you need help and actively looking for it.

- **Level Three:** Engaging in the work and accepting the ups and downs.

- **Level Two:** Showing up in the healing space with an open willingness.

- **Level Four:** Getting creative with how, when, and in what way you design new experiences and programs that will inch you forward.

You can strengthen your process in any of these levels by committing to practices that develop your ability to create change. Learning how to do this is the crux of all healing, which is why this section devotes so much time to helping you realize how to envision change and activate your innate skills that amplify your ability to create results.

FIRST STEPS TO CREATING CHANGE

Wanting change is an internal desire deeply linked to your most true and essential self.

It's critical to respond to the needs of that self with focused attention so that you develop an even greater sense of connection and communication. This is where a fount of healing energy can be generated!

RECIPE FOR DEEPER SELF-CONNECTION

- 1 wish list
- 10 items of priority
- 30 creative ideas
- 5 action plans
- 1 long-term strategy

Fold in the ingredients one by one in the following order:

1. Write out a wish list of ten things you could have, see, or do that would make you feel good about yourself, who you are, the recovery work you're doing, and what it means to be you.

2. Prioritize the items on your list, starting with the most important.

3. Beginning from the top of the list, creatively (on your own or with the input of friends, family, colleagues, or a healing professional) generate three ideas to give yourself what you need to feel supported and cared for in each area.

4. Take your top five wishes and, based on the ideas, make an action plan for following through.

Put in place a long-term process (e.g., what you will do daily, weekly, monthly) for activating a strategy to obtain as many things on the list as you feel ready for.

Reverse-engineer your process.

If someone planted you at the base of a mountain and asked you to leap up to the summit, you'd look at him as if he were crazy. You'd know intuitively that, unless he offered to airlift you to the top, there would be many steps involved in climbing to the highest peak. You'd also know that, in order to be successful, he'd have to give you time to make the trek, plus the right supplies and resources.

In other words, you'd know that there were small experiences that needed to successfully happen to lead up to the big success of climbing the entire mountain. Let's apply that kind of logic to your recovery.

When you have a very clear idea of your recovery's desired outcome(s), plus the actions it requires, then it's time to define a process for achieving it.

Keep the sensation of overwhelm at bay by looking at the end result and then breaking down that picture into small, manageable steps.

> Identify one of your most wanted PTSD healing outcomes. Visualize in your mind or enter in your notebook, journal, or computer all the details of what that end result looks like. Then make a list of all the things that will have to happen for the outcome to be realized. Number each item on the list in the order they must be achieved and then…map out a process for how you will take the first step.

There are a vast number of things you can do to transform who you are, how you feel, and the way in which you live.

Are you ready to do what it takes to create your transformation?

The answer to this question is the most critical piece of information you need. If you are not ready to undertake the work, explorations, or emotions necessary for moving forward, then your first step is to figure out why you don't feel ready and what you need to shift into a place of feeling prepared to move ahead with consistent engagement and participation.

Take some time to deeply and honestly answer the question, "How ready/prepared am I to do what it takes to create my recovery transformation?"

Acknowledging the answer with suspended judgment (and removing any blocks that it illuminates) will allow you to take your first steps toward constructing your own positive and resilient post-trauma identity and PTSD recovery process.

~~~~~

Change happens in small increments over time.

You want to feel better, so you survey the healing landscape and identify a big gesture that you hope will cause big change. Perhaps it's letting go of an old coping habit, or deciding to move more quickly in the healing process you've undertaken. Or you have made an effort to make a change in how you think, feel, act, or behave, and...are dismayed to see it hasn't really changed the overall picture.

Here's a PTSD truth to remember: Zero changes happen in their immediate entirety. All healing change builds up in tiny moments that accumulate into significant outcomes.

As disappointing as it is that the big gestures or the time you put in yield less-than-favorable results, the method behind the madness of the slowness of change can be really profound.

Taking a longer time to practice and create a successful outcome means that, by the time you reap the benefits, *you own them* precisely *because* they didn't happen quickly or easily and because you did have to achieve a type of mastery to attain success.

When this happens, you own the outcomes *for life*. You own the strategy for success and all that you learned while designing it. Plus, now you can use it for future reference in healing, as well as in other places outside PTSD.

Your job in recovery is to make the small increments happen, day after day. Choose one small change that you can put in place today and commit to practicing it daily for the next thirty consecutive days.

~~~~~

Changing your point of view changes what you know, which changes how you act, behave, respond, want, choose, and expect.

Consider how you experience your life after trauma. Are you seeing just a small part of who you are, or are you seeing the whole, larger picture of what it means to be you?

When you live in survival mode, the extreme focus on being safe dramatically limits your point of view. You see only a close-up on survival/coping actions necessary to get through the day and your Survivor Self muddling through it.

Now imagine this: What if you were to pan back and see the rest of yourself and even the world around you in greater specificity?

In such a wide shot, you would find (hidden in the picture's details) aspects of yourself that desire to interact with the outside world in ways irrelevant to survival. You might notice a red baseball cap that reminds you of how good it felt to be the slugger on your Little League team. You might notice the smile of a stranger and feel the sensation of what it would be like to be that comfortable in the world and in yourself. You might notice your reflection as you walk down the street and see that you look different on the outside than you feel on the inside—you look more confident, perhaps, or stronger.

Knowing the potential of these hidden details can change your interpretation of the moment and allow you to tap into the other side of survival mode: life-affirming mode, a place in which being alive is all about the pleasure of feeling good versus the unhappiness of feeling bad.

Practice changing your point of view. Wherever you are, see what colors you notice, what smells you recognize, what sounds

you hear, and what tastes you experience. What do they make
you think, feel, want, or remember that is good, pleasurable,
and hopeful?

~~~~~

**When you treat yourself kindly, you develop an approach to living
that is not fear- or trauma-focused.**

A chief element of PTSD recovery is freeing yourself from a constant sense
of danger. Obviously, work in this area has to do with how you perceive and
interact with the outside world. It also has to do with how you interact with
yourself. When you threaten yourself through abusive thoughts, language,
and ideas, you increase your sensation of danger; this echoes out into your
whole experience of the world, which makes it very hard to shift out of
fearful living.

There are some very simple and powerful ways to develop a kinder
attitude toward yourself:

- **Change your language:** Your internal dialogue is the first place that
  could probably use some attention. Start listening and hear how
  often you use words like *should, have to, ought to,* and *must.* These
  are surefire signs that you're putting negative pressure on yourself.
  Try substituting *want, choose to, would, could, wish,* and *desire* to
  give yourself some more open space in which to live.

- **Choose more fair descriptions:** Notice how often you call yourself
  names or describe yourself (to yourself or others) in unkind and
  unflattering ways. Do you call yourself *stupid, idiotic, pathetic,
  useless, worthless,* or *damaged*? These descriptions are all very
  hurtful and completely untrue. You don't have to love yourself right
  now, but at least be fair: You're doing the best you can, so describe
  yourself that way.

- **Do nice things for yourself:** With your focus on danger/threat,
  recovery/healing, and the challenges of both, you probably don't

take much time to give yourself good experiences. If you had a friend who was feeling down or sick, you'd make a meal, take her to a movie, buy a little present, or do any of a slew of things that would cheer her up. Pampering yourself in that way can lift your spirits and renew your energy.

- **Honor yourself:** This advice is not always easy to take, but really deserves some focus. Having respect for yourself is the foundation for being and becoming the person you most wish to be. Doing this means standing up for yourself; acknowledging that you matter; and understanding and accepting how you feel, think, and behave. It also means asking others to honor you as well by treating you in respectful ways.

Over the next four weeks, implement these options, one per week, until you've activated all four in your daily life.

In default mode, you stay stuck in a feeling of victimhood and powerlessness—exactly where you're trying to get out of!

Living in default mode means you:

- initiate very little
- expend all energy on managing post-trauma symptoms

- focus on responding to what life brings your way
- react defensively
- rarely proactively choose or decide

If you remain in default mode, in the best-case scenario, you will always feel as unhappy as you do today; in the worst-case scenario, you will put yourself in danger and experience future traumas because you did not reclaim control over who you are and how you live.

The key to getting out of default mode is getting into the habit of making choices and taking actions. It's in that sequence that you attain power.

Practice being super-conscious today about how, when, where, in what way, and with whom you make choices and take actions.

For even the most inconsequential choice, say to yourself, "I choose..."

What would make the process of choice feel more comfortable? How can you create those circumstances more often?

~~~~~~

Be conscious, directed, engaged, and connected.

Most people in the world are going about their lives today without actively assessing who they are and who they want to be. They will get up and go through the motions of work and after-work hours by habit, without connecting to their deep truth and purpose.

In your quest for healing, however, you can choose to be even just a tiny iota more conscious and connected to who you are, want to be, and can be than yesterday. In this way, you will turn the tragedy of trauma into the launchpad that transforms you from a creature of unchosen habit to a person who lives a meaningful life from the moment your feet hit the floor in the morning until you go to bed at night.

Pause throughout the day and check in with yourself: What are you thinking, feeling, wanting, and experiencing? Specify each feeling, thought, desire, and experience by describing it through an "I am..." statement.

~~~~~~

Your brain has one primary job: finding proof of what you tell it.

As a matter of fact, your brain is hardwired and genetically programmed for this role. This means you want to be very careful about what you tell it, so that your brain finds proof of the things that are most beneficial to you.

The more you tell your brain the good things you want it to find proof of, the more it can support you in everything you seek to accomplish.

From this day forward, "I can't handle it!" is now on your list of taboo phrases. Instead, every time you hear yourself saying that phrase (either out loud or in your own mind) or even just feeling it, cancel that thought and replace it with, "I am completely capable of handling this." With this reframe, your brain begins to look for *how* you can handle the situation, which helps you transition from fear into action mode.

> Adopt the mantra: "I can handle it!" Every time you feel fear, repeat the phrase and then give yourself three reasons why you know, hope, or suspect that statement is true.

You have within you a mechanism that allows you to understand or know things without conscious thought.

As 88 percent of your brain, your subconscious mind notices and records approximately 20,000,000 bits of environmental stimuli per second. Compare that to the approximate 40,000 bits per second your conscious mind processes as the remaining 12 percent of your brain. From this quick snapshot, you can see that your subconscious mind has access to much more information than your conscious mind in any moment. The significance of this lies in the fact that, when you hear that small voice in your head or feel that feeling you don't understand, you may discount it because your conscious mind can't qualify its accuracy—but your mind is sending you valid and important information. Intuition becomes useful when 100 percent of your brain works together. With so much going on below the surface, you may receive the message to take a particular action without clearly knowing why.

You may challenge it by asking, "Why should I do this?" or "How do I know this is true?"

But there is a better question to ask.

When you receive intuitive messages, forget about why and how; ask instead, "What do you want me to do?"

> Start listening for your intuitive voice. Ask, "What do you want me to do?" and listen for the answer. See how often you can defer to it and follow the instructions you receive.

In every moment, you have the potential to operate from your Ideal or Survivor Self.

You've been more in your Survivor Self for an extended period of time. Being reminded that your Ideal Self (that part of you that is strong, empowered, and able to make good decisions) exists offers an opportunity to stretch the muscle of your Ideal Self in action.

Engaging your Ideal Self means looking through the eyes of the part of you that can be objective, open, deliberate, and willing to observe without evaluating. This doesn't mean you have to live as that part in every moment; it simply means that you are going to make an effort to look through the eyes of that part more often.

> Practice accessing your Ideal Self by suspending judgment in any moment and simply seeing and acknowledging what is.

Stop. Take a step back. Tune into your (inner) self.

Both your mind and body offer healthy, useful information. Developing a habit of checking in with yourself is vital to reclaiming control. The more you trust yourself to be connected to and aware of the accurate messages your mind and body send, the more you will build confidence that you can protect yourself, which is a huge aspect of transformation.

The objective here is to proceed toward what feels good or even just a little bit better. The key to achieving that is becoming aware of what you want or need and honoring it in the moment in which you receive the information.

Six times today, identify a moment when you will work these action steps:

- Ask, "Do I want this?" Listen for the answer.

- Then ask, "What do I want?" Listen for the answer.

- Then ask, "What action can I take to get that?"

While your initial sensory response to a stimulus may not be under your control, your post-response is absolutely within the realm of your choosing.

The following is a generalized and overly simplified model of how emotions begin and evolve. The purpose of the diagram is to introduce you to one simple concept: where and how you can claim control.

EVOLUTION OF EMOTION

STIMULUS
Senses deliver information to brain.

INTERPRETATION
Mind assesses the meaning of the stimuli.

THOUGHT
Ideas form in relation to the meaning.

PHYSIOLOGICAL RESPONSE
Body chemistry registers a response to the ideas.

FEELING
Body sensation registers a response to the chemistry.

IMPULSE TO ACT
Mind and body choose a responsive behavior.

PSYCHOLOGICAL RESPONSE
Mind responds to the meaning of the experience.

The second step—interpretation—is the locus of control. If you learn how to intercept and engage your mind at this early part of the emotional evolution process, it can be particularly effective in managing any emotion (especially anger).

Try this: The next time you have an intense emotion, focus
on identifying your interpretation of the moment you are in.
Then ask, "What interpretation would make me feel a little bit
better?" Shift your focus to create that scenario. (This process
takes practice; accept right now that you will go through a
learning curve to wholly achieve it.)

~~~~~

**Tapping into your sense of being able to succeed in specific situations
strengthens your recovery efforts.**

In any moment, you either feel power*less* or power*ful*. Essentially, this
boils down to the thoughts, "I *can't* handle it!" or "I *can* handle it!"

After trauma, your natural shift to the powerless side of the pendulum
decreases how effectively you create who you are, how you live, how you
feel, and how you recover.

You can begin flipping the sensation of power from -*less* to -*ful* by
embodying these four elements of self-efficacy:

1. Feeling you are able to
   take actions and receive
   positive results

2. Feeling able to keep yourself
   safe and/or protected

3. Living in meaningful
   connection with yourself
   and the world

4. Continuing to develop in
   ways that expand your
   ability to be an agent
   of change, rather than
   constantly being changed by
   (unexpected) events

Choose one of these four areas. What makes you feel powerless
in this category? What would make you feel even just the
slightest bit more powerful in this area? What would have

to happen to create that feeling? How can you create that experience? Who can help?

~~~~~

Your sense of self-worth begins with believing you matter.

Coping with trauma activates psychological survival mechanisms, some of which involve shutting down overwhelming emotions. To feel less grief, fear, and trepidation, you may shift into a place where you feel nothing at all. While doing this allows you to experience less uncomfortable emotions, it also allows you to feel less comfortable and comforting emotions.

In this space, it's normal to begin defining yourself in negative and demeaning terms. This causes you to experience decreased feelings of personal, social, and professional value.

The combined result of these shifts: In the deadened wasteland, nothing matters, not even you, which makes you feel even more undeserving, unfit, unwanted, and unlovable. (These negative beliefs, by the way, are false.)

Transforming out of this place begins with reconnecting to a sensation of what matters about you, for you, and to you.

If you were going to believe that you matter, what would let you know that concept is true? How would you experience that? How can you create that experience today?

~~~~~

Higher self-esteem (an important ingredient in resilience) can regulate emotional distress.

Self-esteem is defined as "confidence in your own worth and abilities." The way to being stronger and more resilient—and reaping the benefits those offer in recovery and brain change—has to do with building yourself up in this area.

In fact, studies prove that self-esteem is reflected in the extent of brain change after trauma and how the brain continues to change despite enormous stress.

If you feel ready to try something new, include any of these options in your daily experience:

- **Set realistic objectives:** It's easy to be down on yourself if you set the bar too high. While it's good to give yourself benchmarks and missions, it's also good to be realistic about what you're capable of achieving right now. Be kind to yourself and set forth ideas for who you are and will be, on any day, that are commensurate with where you are in your recovery process. You can increase your objectives as you move forward, gain strength, and build your confidence and self-trust. *What are some reasonable objectives to have for yourself today, tomorrow, and next week?*

- **Embrace your successes and failures:** First, eliminate the word *failures* and substitute *unexpected outcomes*, because that's what any lack of success is. Then, approach success or its absence as opportunities for exploration and discovery. *Why did the situation work out as you wanted it to? How will you use that information in the future? Why didn't the situation work out as you wanted it to? How will you use that information in the future?*

- **Acknowledge your positive qualities:** After trauma, it's easy to find things to despise about who you are and how you behave, but the truth is that there's a whole you, too. This means that what trauma highlights about you is only a *part* of the entire you that you are. Recovery benefits from your recognizing there are good things about you. *If you had to list five good things about you, what would they be?*

- **Identify what you're good at and do it often:** Trauma and coping with post-trauma symptoms disconnects you from your real-world strengths. With all your time and energy spent on managing, you can easily forget to keep up skills unrelated to survival. But those skills can help you transition through trauma and out the other side where they, more than your trauma skills, will serve to evolve you and your life long-term. *What are you good at? How often do you allow yourself to engage in that activity?*

- **Share your gifts (qualities, strengths, skills) with others:** Yes, isolation feels good, but doing something that makes someone else feel good feels even better (and releases serotonin, a mood-enhancing hormone). You've got skills that are useful to others. Whether that's personal or professional, paid or volunteer, find ways and times to give something good about you to someone else. Not only does being helpful feel pleasurable, but this simple practice also puts you in touch with a part of the whole you that, if you continue to connect, can help bridge you through the post-trauma transition. *What are you good at? Who could use some help in that way?*

This week, test each of the preceding options more than once to jump-start your self-esteem growth.

Your beliefs drive 100 percent of your behavior.

Beliefs are built on your acceptance of the truth of a particular statement. Everything you do, see, feel, experience, and claim is important based on your belief system.

The tricky thing about beliefs is that they operate below your level of consciousness. While beliefs are available to your conscious scrutiny—meaning you can be 100 percent aware of and interactive with them—they operate like habits: driving you to do things without thinking about it or making a conscious choice to take an action. When you behave from unquestioned beliefs, you create an identity and experiences around the (false) negative beliefs you hold.

Engaging your belief-wrangling capabilities is crucial to reclaiming control. While beliefs operate at lightning speed, the truth is you are stronger, faster, and more effective than any belief—if you decide to intervene. Beliefs can cause chaos, but when you actively identify and transform them, you shift out of a negative belief cycle and into a more supportive method of achieving your well-being and desires.

> What belief do you lack today that you wish you had? In your notebook, journal, or computer, complete this statement:
>
> "I wish I believed…"
>
> What would have to happen for you to believe that? How can you find or create proof that would get you just a little closer to embracing that belief?

~~~~~~

The theme of connection/reconnection runs throughout the recovery process in myriad ways.

Trauma blows up the train tracks of your life. Recovery challenges you to reconnect those tracks so that the train can start running again on a consistent schedule. While there are many different opportunities to practice connection and reconnection, they all orbit like moons around three main planets: yourself, others, and the world.

Often, reconnection requires combining choices about who you are with self-creating actions—plus courageously rejecting the ideas of others in favor of beliefs and identity-building-blocks that you authentically value.

Internally, you'll learn to connect the past with the present, and then connect the future, while linking your splintered selves into one expansive entity. Externally, you'll connect to people, places, and experiences.

TEN TOP AREAS OF (RE)CONNECTION IN PTSD RECOVERY:

- Your fragmented parts to your whole self
- Your mind to your body
- Your values to your lifestyle

- Your trauma story to post-trauma truth

- Present to the future

- Past to the present

- You to the present

- Friends to the new you

- Family to the new you

- Your self to yourself

Choose one of these areas and imagine what steps you would have to take to reach the outcome of (re)connection. Identify three ways you can begin creating that experience.

~~~~~~

Through the process of struggling with adversity, you have the opportunity to upshift to a higher level of functioning.

As a human, you have a need to understand, process, integrate, and assign meaning to every experience. After trauma, you look back and develop stories to explain what you have survived. Those stories can lead you into terrific post-traumatic growth ("I'm incredibly strong to have been able to survive that!") or down a path of post-traumatic stress ("It's entirely my fault that this awful thing happened to me"). Post-traumatic growth is better, don't you agree?

There are five main areas of positive post-traumatic development:

- Perceived changes in self

- Closer family relationships

- Changed philosophy in life

- Better perspective on life

- Strengthened belief system

Exploring your own evolution in these areas—either in the past or what you plan for the future—offers five keys to resilience that are completely available to you at any time.

In which categories have you experienced post-traumatic growth? How do you know? In what positive way will that change your response to future experiences?

~~~~~

Everything you need to address and/or handle will wait.

The anxiety of the PTSD lifestyle easily drips into the recovery process; your Survivor Self worries, fears, and builds up anxiety to such a point that some days just make you want to turn your face away from the difficulties, the disturbances, and all the discomfort that goes along with recovery.

So, you know what? Give yourself an opportunity to do that! Taking a break to release the tension—even to the point of pretending that PTSD doesn't exist in your world—is a great way to let off steam; restore energy; open up new creativity; and refresh your dedication, commitment, and ability to process.

Pick a time this week to say, "Not today!" Your brain thrives on diverse experiences. Get out of your habitual schedule and give yourself a break by doing something you never do.

~~~~~

Regardless of what happened in the past, it's time to turn on your positivity bias in the present.

Naturally, you scan for danger and threat. In fact, you were born with a negativity bias, a process by which your brain more easily recalls negative experiences than positive ones. The negativity bias is how your brain learns and how it keeps you safe. Right now, your negativity bias is working overtime.

With such a narrow scope of vision, the PTSD lifestyle and perspective become incredibly reactive. However, when you use your ability to notice positive things, you widen your perspective in small, safe, manageable, and even comfortable ways. The result: Your brain (re)learns that there's more to life than outrunning the tigers; it learns to develop a counter-balanced positivity bias.

To begin exploring your positivity bias, try noticing the good things that happen in a day. With a PTSD-centric focus, this might begin by noticing and appreciating that you coped well enough to quell a panic attack more quickly than usual, or you actually slept without a nightmare.

See the positive, observe, note, and move on.

> Today, make an effort to follow this four-step process and notice your response. Repeat the process every day for a week and observe your response. Continue for thirty consecutive days and examine the difference in how you think, feel, see, and experience the world.

~~~~~

Give yourself what you want.

In the PTSD mindset and lifestyle, you rarely give yourself what you want. Focusing on survival means you spent your energy entirely on giving yourself what you "need," which is driven by a lot of "what if " thinking related to your safety, external threats, and future dangers.

Healing, however, offers an opportunity for you to give yourself what's good for you. That is, to honor what you intuitively feel you want in any moment. In this way, recovery provides a path back to loving yourself and living in a way that honors the You you most want to be.

> Imagine there's a part of you that has been neglected for a very long time. What does she want? What would make her happy? How can you give her that today? How can you do that in more and more healthy ways every day?

Tweet happiness.

You receive back in energy and experience what you put out into the world. If you face each day with the intention to lead from a place of pain, anger, grief, loss, resentment, brokenness, hopelessness, and fear, then that's what the world will send back to you.

Check in with yourself. What kind of experience do you want to have in the world?

Part of healing is reclaiming a sense of your own power. One way to do this is to create the world and environment in which you wish to live.

Feel better about yourself and bring to yourself more positive experiences by being a voice of compassion in someone else's pain, offering someone a ray of hope in an otherwise dreary day, posting an inspirational quote on social media, or volunteering for an organization that's meaningful to you.

There is a positive side to who you are. (In fact, that's the part of you that picked up this book.) Engage with that part; embrace and embody it. Spend time letting it lead you.

> Practice accessing your more hopeful self. Tweet something hopeful about PTSD recovery (i.e., a coping mechanism that helps you, progress you've made, supportive information) to @ChangeYouChoose #healmyptsd.

HOW TO GAIN (AND KEEP) MOMENTUM

Being intentional is one of the strongest tools in PTSD recovery.

If you research how to create intentions, you'll find advice that caters to the idea of creating affirmations—which is great. However, the idea suggested here is a bit different.

For the purposes of your recovery process, an intention (1) creates specificity about what you want, (2) combines that with why it's important to you, and then (3) identifies what you will receive by having that experience. All together, this creates focus for your mind, your brain, and your emotions.

You can use this equation for any type of intention by asking yourself three important questions:

- What do I want?
- What will I gain by having it?
- Why do I want that?

What does this look like for you in the area of healing? Ask yourself the three questions as they relate to your recovery process. Write out as many details as possible for each answer. Then string them together into a full composite statement that looks like this:

"I want...because...so that..."

Once you set an intention, it can act as a compass guiding you through every moment. Your intention may be as long or short as you feel comfortable with. It's your intention, so you can do whatever you like with it!

Practice using this process to create three intentions this week.

When you live in the present, you are more in control, more connected, more effective, and more in alignment with who you are, what you're doing, and who you want to be.

One trick to staying in the present moment is to remember the spirit of your intention.

For every experience you are about to have (whether that's eating a slice of pizza or going out with friends), before you enter the experience, ask yourself: "How do I want to feel, think, and behave during this activity?"

Develop your intention using the guidelines from the previous exercise, and then use the following three questions to help you achieve your mission:

- What will have to happen for me to implement this intention?

- What will I need to be able to take those actions?

- Who can help me achieve this intention?

How purposefully are you living? For the next twenty-four hours, pause and ask yourself, "What do I want this experience to be like?" before you engage in any activity. Whether it's brushing your teeth or meeting someone for a meal, check in with yourself, identify your intention, choose three actions you need to take to achieve that purpose, and then find ways to build them into your experience.

Being intentional with your life starts with being intentional in the small moments.

Start looking for moments that have little stress as a way to ease yourself into practicing purpose. When you make a habit of being intentional in the easy moments, you build your purpose muscle so that it kicks in even in the more stressful times of your life.

In this way, living with purpose can become a terrific tool for grounding and centering yourself in both good and challenging moments. All it takes is two things:

1. **Create purpose.** In any moment or for any experience, pause and complete this statement:

   "For this moment/experience, I intend to..."

   Holding onto this sentence throughout the experience can help you stay on track and focused in making decisions and choosing behaviors.

2. **Make the decision to commit.** Defining your purpose is only half the equation. You must dedicate yourself to the *consistent* choices and actions required to make the existence of that purpose a priority. Committing can come in the form of a promise to yourself, or even to someone else holding you accountable.

Find three small moments today in which to practice being intentional by developing and acting on your purpose.

~~~~~~

Implementing purpose in PTSD recovery can help provide focus, direction, and balance.

Healing from trauma can feel like a tornado that darkens the sky and then whips up a wind that upsets and rearranges your entire landscape, carrying off dear and important objects along the way. In response, you probably feel scattered and fragmented, plus spend a lot of time thinking about what happened in the past and how unhappy you are with your situation in the present.

With all of that going on, PTSD typically prevents you from imagining you're going to have a normal future. When you look ahead, you usually see danger, threat, and disappointment. Those flooding pressures create a narrow perspective: PTSD recovery is the looming focus; forcing yourself through it is your biggest aim.

When your focus and feeling are so negatively biased, it can become hard to breathe, let alone heal. Shifting to an approach that fuels rather than exhausts you can open up more energy and provide momentum. Updating your PTSD recovery purpose can help in exactly this way.

Take a look at the difference in these two purpose statements:

- "My purpose is to fix my broken self if it kills me!"

vs.

- "My purpose is to lovingly and with self-compassion keep seeking ways to feel better until I am happy with who I am and how I live and do so in a state of symptom-free calm and security."

Being proactive about defining your purpose (rather than letting your PTSD brain choose it for you) alters your recovery approach; which alters your experience; which changes your thoughts, feelings, behaviors, beliefs, and fears. All of this adds up to big wins in recovery.

> Try creating your PTSD recovery purpose. What you enter in your notebook, journal, or computer will change with time and as you progress and grow.
>
> "My PTSD recovery purpose is..."

There are many ways to apply the idea of purpose to your life outside healing.

You can apply purpose (your intention) in numerous ways that have zero to do with PTSD recovery. This point is extremely relevant for the following reasons:

1. **While you're recovering, you're also living in the world outside PTSD.** You have relationships, commitments, and responsibilities. Defining your purpose in these areas helps maintain your connection to how you want to show up for and sustain these connections despite PTSD challenges.

2. **During recovery, you're simultaneously creating the person you will be when PTSD is a thing of the past.** While your non-recovery-related purpose(s) will change as you evolve, having an eye on them provides balance because it links you from your present to your future. In this way it widens your perspective and reminds you that future moments exist; plus you will have the choice of creating them.

What is your purpose for your life after PTSD? In your notebook, journal, or computer, define your purpose (as you see it today or what you hope it will be) in the following areas:

- "My purpose for who I am/will be is…"

- "My purpose for how I live/will live is…"

- "My purpose for the work I do/will do is…"

- "My purpose for how I experience/will experience the world is…"

Add your own areas as they occur to you.

$\sim\sim$

Clarity is safety.

It's common through the recovery process to feel frightened as you see, feel, and hear yourself change. You may not recognize yourself, or you may feel like an imposter. Coming back into your body and mind and restoring your sense of self after a long hiatus is a glorious transition, but it can also be very disconcerting.

The clearer you are on what's happening and why you're engaging in it, the stronger and more capable you become, and the more the world and your place in it dramatically alter. The foundation of this clarity lies in your beliefs, wants, desires, wishes, objectives, and intentions. The more clarity you have in these areas, the more control you achieve over who you are and who you will become. All together, this translates into more safety during the recovery process and beyond.

When you feel transformational discomfort, refocus your clarity. Ask yourself:

- What am I hoping to achieve in this moment?

- Why is this important to me?

- How, specifically, will this create positive outcomes in my life?

Then take a comfortable action to deepen your commitment and further dedicate yourself to this process.

~~~~

Being clear on what you dislike about yourself opens opportunities for change.

What do you dislike about who you are today?

On the surface, this seems like an easy question to answer. Statements come to mind like, "I hate that I'm anxious. I hate that I don't trust. I hate that I can't control my anger. I hate that I don't have enough money." While these answers are extremely relevant, they represent the most superficial layer of what you know and think about yourself. Deep change comes from understanding why you are who you are.

For example, if you hate that you get angry, then it will help to know what thoughts (e.g., fears) create that feeling in you. Behind each thought is a belief, plus an interpretation of a situation that causes the disturbing thought. Which thoughts, specifically, make you feel angry? What beliefs lead to the creation of your angry feelings? The statement "I hate that I can't control my anger" might be masking the thought "I hate that I don't follow through on the decisions I make about learning to control my emotions," which might come from the belief "I'm not capable of being in control." Now we're getting somewhere!

While the original statement can lead to a decision to take an anger management class, the second statement addresses what stops you from being who you want to be: someone who follows through. The third statement identifies why you don't follow through: You believe you can't succeed. With this knowledge, you can begin working to shift from a negative into a positive belief about the possibility for success, which will lead to a higher percentage of follow-through, which leads to significant changes in what you dislike about yourself so that you move closer to who you would like to be.

The next time you notice something about yourself that you dislike, ask:

- What feeling prompted me to do that?

- What interpretation of myself, others, or the world caused that feeling?

- What thought created that response?

- What belief drives that kind of thinking?

- What would I prefer to do?

- What would have to change so that preference is my response?

- How can I make that happen?

The number-one healing word is...What.

To achieve your healing intention, recovery requires a lot of creation. Here's the catch: You can create only what you can actually or imaginatively see, feel, hear, taste, or smell. The cues from your senses instill in your imagination an idea; from there, you move toward it, pulled by desire, longing, expectation, vision, and belief.

What kind of vision do you have for your healing process?

After trauma, clarity can be scarce. The PTSD brain fog, lack of sleep, dysregulated emotions, and triggers can make it extremely hard to think, much less think straight to an image or vision of what you want your healed self and circumstances to be. That's why it's so important and useful to make *What* your number-one go-to word.

Using *What* in both healing and living can help clarify yourself, your world, and the other people in it. Constantly question yourself and your experiences. Push yourself to define the most inconsequential items, issues, and experiences so that you develop an ability to acutely define the more meaningful and affecting ones.

Incorporating *What* into your constant vocabulary as a question ("What do I want?") or statement ("What I want is...") allows you to become super-present about your experience(s), other people's actions, and aspects of the world. The extra clarity can lead you to new choices and empowered actions.

> This week, play around with asking yourself, "What?" as often as possible. Use it in a slew of different ways, from "What is this about?" to "What do I want?" to "What does this feeling come from?" Following each question, use "What" in an action statement, e.g., "What I'm choosing to do is..."

If there is one question to ask yourself in recovery, this is the one: "What's one small thing I can do today?"

You look up at the mountain of healing and think, "No way!" True, from the bottom, it can seem as if that's a long, steep trek, and you'd be a fool to even wish you might make it to the top.

But people make it to the top all the time. Here's their secret: They do it slowly, step by step. Each step they take is geared to a small choice, action, and outcome.

When you apply to your recovery every day (and follow through on) the one philosophy held in the question "What's one small thing I can do today?" you push forward in constant motion at a pace that is manageable.

> Change starts in the moment you choose it. What is one small thing you can do today that will move you forward in your quest to cope and heal?

Developing your ability to make decisions puts you in touch daily with a strong success motivator: your "I want" driver.

The more you reward this driver, the more often it will engage with you. Constructing your post-trauma identity absolutely hinges on this pillar. To live an active, illuminated, and engaged life that feels good to you requires recognition and delivery of what you want in all arenas of your life, including self-definition; career; relationships; finances; health and wellness; rest and relaxation; and spiritual, family, and religious aspects.

The greatest characteristic of this core element is how easy it is to implement. You can begin developing your decision-making process and "I choose" habit with small things like, "I choose to have a burger for lunch." Or, "I choose not to watch this movie." While you train yourself to look, wait for, and expect your choices, this habit will simultaneously and elegantly announce to those around you that you are assuming a more empowered role.

For a full day, practice saying "I want" all day. Apply that prefix phrase down to the tiniest choice you make. Notice the difference between how you feel when you first say it at the beginning of the day and how you feel by the end of the day. What has changed?

~~~~~

Your brain naturally turns on motivation when you allow it to diversify its experiences.

Motivation is your reason for behaving or acting in a certain way. When it is tied to your positive desires, dreams, and wants, it can infuse your recovery with terrific momentum.

Try any of these ways to tap into a sense of motivation:

- **Experience:** Feeling good for even just twenty seconds has been scientifically proven to create new neural pathways. When you allow yourself to be open to experiences that feel good, you give yourself permission to engage in your brain's powerful neuronal connection processes while at the same time forming new memories that offer you insight into what's truly possible for you to feel. Often, trauma trains you to think your emotional capability has been deadened. Truthfully, it's waiting for a reason to reengage. The more you feel good, the more you will want to feel good, and the more you will naturally feel compelled to take even the tiniest action that will help you achieve that feeling again and again and again.

- **Connection:** In conversation with a group, therapist, or close and trusted friend, you can observe, be with, and share your experience of a motivating moment; your experience of accessing what drives you to achieve something. Doing this extends the feeling, reduces isolation, expands your experience, deepens the neural pathways it creates, and connects you to a secure sense of your own humanness, which can profoundly activate courage, compassion, and kindness.

- **Desire:** Desire acts as a key motivator for any action. Propelling you toward a much-wanted outcome, it activates your reward-seeking brain and encourages your choices in the direction of what is most important to you. You can amp up the power of motivation in your life by becoming aware of how much you want something and why it matters. Spend some time sitting with your desire; feel its presence; imagine the feeling you'll have when you get what you want; close your eyes and watch the scene unfold as you receive what you desire.

Pick one of these options. Then test how you can utilize it today, and share your experience with someone else.

~~~~

Trusting yourself is a learnable skill.

Lacking self-trust is a normal by-product of shock, surprise, and powerlessness. Whether you were five months or fifty years old at the time of your trauma, losing your ability to trust yourself—and finding ways to get it back—is a common theme in trauma and PTSD recovery.

SELF-TRUST = CONTROL

You weren't born with the ability to trust yourself. You gained that self-supporting trait through experiences that let you see that you know you will..., you can..., and you are....

You lost (aspects of) that skill due to an experience that seemed to teach you the opposite—that you couldn't be trusted in some way. Maybe you lost faith in your ability to appropriately respond to threat, judge people, or defend or protect yourself. However the loss occurred, a "skill" is nothing more than the learned ability to do something. With a little bit of practice and conscious focus, you can (re)develop self-trust and use it as a support system for your recovery.

To get headed in the right direction, follow these three steps:

1. **Define what it means to trust yourself.** Before you can develop a skill, you need to know what, exactly, you're trying to do. Take some time to get very clear on what "self-trust" means to you. Draft a full definition, make a list of ideas, or simply organize your thoughts in terms of truths. Ask: "If I had self-trust, what would be true about me?"

2. **Identify how you would know that you trust yourself.** To reach the end result, you need to know what signs to look for that signify success. Ask yourself: when I have self-trust...

   - How will I know?
   - What will I feel?
   - What will I hear in my head that recognizes the presence of self-trust?
   - What will I see that's different about me?
   - What kinds of actions will I take?
   - What kinds of behavior will I engage in?

   For a few moments, think ahead and imagine you have achieved self-trust; what will be different about you and your life?

3. **Create opportunities to practice behaving in those ways.** The only way to develop self-trust is to engage in situations that allow you to flex your self-trust muscle. Action: Based on your answers to the questions in the first two steps, seek out opportunities that allow you to define and implement a self-trust process and practice it. Start with small, inconsequential moments. Then build up to big ones.

In what areas do you feel a lack of trust in yourself? Make a full list. Then prioritize the items from most to least important today. Starting at the top of the list, identify what would have to change for you to trust yourself more in this area.

Develop a plan to create that outcome: What steps do you have to take? Who can help?

~~~~~~

Fan your inner flame.

Part of recovery means building back a sense of self-confidence—belief in your ability to take care of yourself, manage your world, and protect your safety. The key to (re)building confidence lies in believing that your inner flame (your Core Self) actually exists. More than that: It can brightly burn, shine, and flicker in ways that help you reclaim your life, your world, and mostly importantly, your full self.

1. **Give yourself small, achievable objectives in which you can succeed.** The more you build up a track record of success, the more you will automatically believe in your ability to accomplish things.

2. **Get in touch with things you do well.** Spend more time doing things that make you feel good about your capabilities so that you are often (daily!) in touch with how your actions lead to positive outcomes.

3. **Be helpful to someone else.** Sometimes we're much better at helping others than ourselves; this can be a great place to build up feelings of strength and self-efficacy that can be used for your own benefit later.

There are specific actions you can take to rebuild your self-confidence. While it's a process that happens slowly, these ideas can get you going today.

~~~~~~~

While it helps to embrace and embody your feelings, it's also beneficial to actively transform them.

When you deliberately process and alter a feeling, you exercise your power to transition from disturbance to a less distressing emotion. Transforming your perception of a feeling changes how your mind associates, records, and responds to it. Accomplishing this puts space between what you feel and how your mind represents it.

You have the freedom and every right to make the decision to engage in this process. Whereas prior to the trauma your process of transforming emotions may have been more natural—you didn't have to think about it— today you will have to consciously decide to genuinely affect it. Doing this in small increments allows you to test how it feels, how to tweak your process, and how to expand inside yourself to make room for new integration and the feelings it provides.

Right now, welcome in a disturbing feeling about the person you have become because of trauma and PTSD.

Imagine you can see this feeling in a big picture in the center of the screen of your mind. (This can be a literal picture or something symbolic.)

Note: *You may not receive any picture at all; that's okay. If that's the case, then throughout this exercise, use the feeling and imagine placing it where instructed.*

Now call up some small aspect of what you love about who you were or could have been yesterday. See this aspect in a small picture in a low corner on the same screen in your mind.

Then swap the pictures: Shrink the big one down and enlarge the small one to a great size.

Now darken the small picture so that it's all black. Then let it fade entirely.

Turn up the light on the remaining picture of the good element about you. Examine, appreciate, and savor it.

Make the deliberate choice to embody, embrace, and exhibit this element today.

~~~~~

Decide your response to the impact of the past on your daily experience.

During your trauma, you were powerless, but you are powerful now. Being powerful means you have choices—which you do—and the opportunity to be effective every second. Even in the midst of troubling symptoms, you have the choice of how you will respond in the moment.

You can practice exercising control with this process:

1. Bring up an uncomfortable feeling/memory.

2. Be with it; you are a room with endless space to hold this feeling/memory.

3. Recognize and understand how the feeling/memory makes you feel and why; it's a reasonable response.

4. Release the feeling as best you can: Imagine some action of letting go (for example, it's a puddle of water and evaporates; it's a balloon and you release the string; it's a liquid that pours out of a pitcher).

5. Imagine that whatever part(s) of your body most holds this feeling opens and, like any type of liquid or viscous material, the feeling spills out (focus on this step for however long it takes), leaving behind an empty space.

6. Into the empty space, put or pour a good-feeling, loving, happy, joyful, hopeful, or other notably good memory.

Practice this process multiple times with one feeling/memory to lessen its charge. Or use this method as a way to quell random feelings/memories that unexpectedly arise.

~~~~~

Slowing down can make you more flexible, resilient, and able to appropriately respond to true danger.

When you don't feel good, it's absolutely normal to try to get better as quickly as possible, even if that means rushing your recovery. The problem is that, when you rush healing, you don't give yourself a chance to truly own it. By skipping steps and running ahead, you leave behind work that needs to be done to help you maintain your gains over a long period of time.

Survivors who make the most progress are willing to take *one step at a time*. This means taking the time to make choices, reflect, understand, and appreciate what you need, have done, and are doing.

Taking your time also gives you the opportunity to see and feel your own power exerting itself, coming forward more and more as you take actions that ensure your safety, wholeness, and happiness. These are the kinds of healing processes that last.

In what area of your healing are you trying to push forward too fast? This week, take some conscious steps to slow down.

~~~~~

Self-assessments are a natural part of the PTSD recovery process.

Whether that's assessing how to follow through on your objectives, what you've learned and how you've changed, or how others view your behavior, taking a step back to see what's working and what isn't (plus how to tweak things to go more smoothly and bring the outcomes you seek) is both a natural pit stop and a necessary way to reclaim, restore, and reconnect to your most essential and best self.

One way to do this is to take a full assessment of your scramble for post-trauma control. What are the pros and cons? How much is all of this behavior making you feel worse instead of better? How much is it costing you things that are important to you?

> Today, stop everything and make a list of all your coping mechanisms—you know, the ones you've developed to help you feel safe and/or in control. In one column, write out as many as you can think of. In another column, write out in specific detail what negative impact they have on your (daily) life. Prioritize from most impact to least. Starting with the behavior that has the most impact, develop an intention for starting to transform and reduce it. Use the exercises on page 149 as a guide.

Take a step back.

Sometimes what can really help you see how to move forward is taking a step back. That is, taking a step back out of the picture of your life and looking into it, seeing yourself from a distance, so that you can observe what's going on from the point of view of your thoughts, outside the emotion. From this distance, it's often possible to transform emotions and see creative solutions to many problems that, when you're in the middle of them, elude you.

> Try this: Close your eyes and think (just for a second) of something you're afraid of. Allow a picture of it to form in your mind. That might be a literal picture, a symbol, or the colorful essence of the feeling. Notice how close it looks and feels. Notice how present it seems, as if you could just reach out and touch it—or worse; it could touch you.

Now imagine you can take a ginormous step back out of the picture so that you can see yourself in it. Then take another step back and perhaps another (if it feels okay, keep going as far back as it takes to feel better).

Then notice: How does that change the feeling of fear? How does that change the way you feel about yourself? How does that alter your sense of being in or out of control?

With this new perspective and sensation come new choices that lead to new actions. What are they? Use any aspect of this exercise any time to help lessen intense feelings.

When you're safe and it feels appropriate, respectfully stand your ground.

As you make more and more choices driven by what you want, the initial response from others may be unreceptive. They may challenge you, saying that you don't really know what you want, or that they can make better decisions than you do. For some time, that may have been true, but if you are going to heal, you are going to have to reclaim your ability to make wise decisions for yourself and have others regard and accept them.

While you can be respectful of another's feelings, you can equally respect your own journey and the changes it requires you to make. The bolder you become in your decisions, the more you may have to explain your actions to others. Take these moments as opportunities to practice both deferring to your intuition when choosing how, when, where, and in what way to express yourself and using strong statements to make your points.

The natural challenges these situations present offer you opportunities to commit even more deeply to your growth, health, life, and recovery. They are moments ripe with the chance to say, "I choose to become who I really want to be," and stand by that through all of the uncomfortable—and liberating— moments that follow.

This exercise may just be the simplest in the whole book! When making any decision (small or large), follow this process:

- Pause.

- Take a step back.

- Reflect on what you want.

- Assess your options for successfully acquiring it.

- Make a decision by saying out loud, "I choose..."

- Take the appropriate action to bring to yourself exactly what you want.

Use the past to your advantage.

Throughout recovery, you can use the past as stepping stones in crossing the river of healing: Each stone of the past grounds you in an understanding of the person you used to be or could have been. It tethers you to a sense of your values today and your ever-evolving sense of what is right or wrong, or what you do/don't want in your life, and can be used to pull you forward to the new shore of recovery.

The next time your healing process requires you to look back, see how these elements show up in the memory:

- What good quality does that moment show about you?

- What courageous element do you exhibit in that moment?

- Name three things you admire about yourself in that moment.

- Notice how those three qualities show up in your current self.

- Identify one way you can exhibit each of those qualities today.

~~~~~~

Pull yourself forward.

You have learned important lessons about yourself and what it means to be you, plus how you can and will choose who you are, how you live, and how you show up in the world. Supporting all of that is this:

At any time, you can discover an aspect of the you of yesterday (or the you you wish you'd had a chance to be)—a behavior, thought, action, dream, wish, or feeling—that resonates with you today. This means that, at any time, you can identify something of important resonance in the past that you wish to bring forward into your present. Once you recognize this idea and feel the tug of it, the next step is to put in place a plan to pull this element into your Now.

The following exercise may feel strange; stay open to the process so that you receive the benefit of the end result.

Pause; take a step back; reflect on who you are today; assess what it means to be you; set aside what you don't like and recognize the positive outcomes trauma has brought into who you are.

Answer these questions in your notebook, journal, or computer:

- What healthy things have you discovered about yourself?

- What positive qualities, strengths, and capabilities has trauma showed you that you possess?

- How will they serve you going forward?

- How can you apply them to your healing process?

For each item you discover, develop a plan for how you can embody and substantially employ it in your life today.

~~~

Activating your ability to make choices grounds and anchors you in the center of your own universe.

In that space, you accept accountability and responsibility for the present and future; with that action, you step into yourself instead of stepping out (and handing off your power to trauma).

Take a look back over the past twenty-four hours. What choices have you made? Are you happy with those choices? Did they feel like choices? What and how would you have chosen differently? What would you have to do next time for things to go the way you would choose?

Bringing your awareness to the many choices you are constantly making develops your focus to notice choices, which opens the opportunity to begin more actively participating in consciously making them.

Think ahead into the next few hours. What choices do you want to make about what you do and how you experience it? Jot down some notes in your notebook, journal, or computer, including ideas for who can help you (and how you will) make sure these are the choices you actually make.

Share these notes with someone who will help you follow through. This can be a real person, or even your Ideal Self.

~~~

Choose to respond instead of react.

Your Survivor Self is dominated by your more deep and interior brain structures that recognize threat, plus the reward system of your midbrain. That self focuses on short-term gratification, the smaller picture, and it desperately tries to avoid pain and conflict. The desire to avoid pain often causes your Survivor Self to suggest doing what's *not* in your best interest in the long term.

Starting today, however, you can choose to make small changes that add up to large alterations in your approach to moving through any moment. When you *respond* (with a carefully thought out, ruled-by-reason action) instead of *react* (with an impulsively decided, ruled-by-emotion action), you begin reclaiming a sense of your power.

Achieving this happens over time. You can start by putting in place this six-step process:

1. **Pause:** Stop what you're doing entirely; freeze the frame of the moment.

2. **Take a step back:** Breathe in and imagine putting space between you and the situation.

3. **Assess:** Notice the facts (not your feelings) of the moment.

4. **Reflect:** Objectively (not according to your feelings) interpret the facts.

5. **Choose:** Identify what you want or need in the moment.

6. **Act:** Behave in a way that moves you closer to what you want or need.

Putting in place any new habit takes time to finesse. Practice the preceding six steps in simple, low-stress moments today to get yourself used to the thought process before applying to more high-stress situations.

Being aware of holding a feeling inside you allows you to see the power you contain: You are bigger than the emotion.

When you challenge your mind to hold two intense and opposite emotions at the same time, one will win out. Through such a practice, you teach your brain to change. Holding the positive and negative together (and then deliberately allowing the positive to become dominant) trains your brain where to place its focus and attention.

There's another bonus to this idea: When you bring up the bad and then infuse yourself with good until the good is what becomes dominant, you are actually putting a good feeling into the bad-feeling neural network. This helps the memory reconsolidate into a deep implicit (unconscious and habitual) memory system imbued with positive associations.

You have the potential to comfortably and consciously feel. You also have the potential to learn how to hold yourself together while embodying any disturbing feeling.

Practice this idea with slightly disturbing memories/feelings (not the absolute core of your trauma):

- Take out a memory that makes you feel uncomfortable. Imagine holding it in the palm of one hand.

- In the other hand, imagine a good memory appears. Allow it to be held comfortably in your palm.

- Imagine shifting your hands up and down to feel the weight of each memory. Feel both the bad and the good equally. Notice which one feels heavier and which feels lighter.

- Now focus on the uncomfortable memory and imagine that, just because you bring your attention there, it begins to shrink—let it shrink down as far as it will go.

- Then focus on the good feeling/memory and imagine it begins to expand and grow bigger. Allow your senses to experience what that means in terms of what you see, smell, taste, feel, and hear. The more the memory grows, the more you want it to grow so that it completely consumes your full attention.

- Shift your hands up and down, feeling how the presence of each idea has changed. Choose the one you prefer by holding that hand higher than the other.

- Now bring both hands together and imagine that the good feeling absorbs the bad feeling into it.

- Bring your hands to your chest and place them palms down over your heart.

- Take a deep breath in; focus on this new feeling for as long as you wish to hold the pose.

~~~~

Engage the power of taking a break!

Sometimes moving forward in healing means working really, really hard and long on one aspect until you crack the code to it. Other times, *not working at all* can lead to enormous breakthroughs. Here's why:

Your brain needs downtime to sort through, sift, organize, and integrate information. Also, your brain thrives and grows on diversity. The broader a variety of experiences you give it, the more happily it functions and grows. From the scientific perspective, research proves that taking a break dramatically improves creativity (legend has it Einstein conceived of the theory of relativity while riding a bike!).

Taking a break in recovery can give you perspective, renewed creativity, and clarity that allows you to move forward in an unexpected but powerful way.

Lay down that heavy trauma backpack today and do something that offers your mind a new, fun, exciting experience. Make a list of possible break/diverse experience options in your notebook, journal, or computer, and refer back to it any time you need some fresh ideas. Ask friends and family to add their suggestions!

PART FOUR

CREATE YOUR NEW IDENTITY

Your PTSD self is a small part of the larger you. True, right now you might feel as though your PTSD self is the *only* you, but that's a false vision created by symptoms.

Deep healing begins with a reconnection to the you that you really are—the New You that encompasses all of the PTSD You while integrating it into the rest of who you are.

This section helps you release the desire to look back to the person you used to be or to regret that trauma never allowed you to have a "before" self. Starting as soon as you turn this page, you will be developing the New You from a perspective that encompasses not only who you were or could have been, but also, even more importantly, who you want to, can, and will become.

PTSD is a mask you've been wearing for many months. It's time to take off that mask and get reacquainted with (and redesign) the image beneath it.

THE ROLE OF IDENTITY IN PTSD RECOVERY

Trauma changes you.

The question "Who am I now?" is one every survivor must face. There is no easy answer. Discovering the New You is equally challenging whether you knew who you were before trauma or not. Here's why.

Even if you have a self to remember, you cannot go back to that self; the most you can do is bring elements of that self forward. So everyone is in the same boat when it comes to creating a post-trauma identity—it starts with who you are today and expands as you discover more and more of who you want to be tomorrow.

Important to remember: Who you were or didn't have a chance to be is only one of many facets of who you are today, but it isn't the sole factor deciding who you can become.

How have you changed or been stunted because of your trauma? Take some time to dig below the surface answer. What bothers you about the changes or lack of growth and development?

Answering these questions lets you know what you value, which lets you know what needs to be reclaimed or developed to create a satisfying post-trauma self.

~~~~

Post-trauma distortions cloud the truth of who you are.

When your life, parts of yourself, and your deep internal connection are altered or damaged (immediately or gradually over time) after a trauma, the inevitable result is that you lose healthy parameters for your perspective. You see yourself as small, alone, and without context. You recognize only the part of you carrying the wounds of trauma, a fractional sliver of your whole self.

Having access to only the small picture of yourself defines the boundaries in which you live, places restrictions on what's possible, and imposes limits on desires. It's like living in a maze and seeing only the walls right in front of your face.

What about the larger context of the world? Does it exist? Is it still available to you? The answer, of course, is, yes—but you have to look for it.

> Identify five beliefs (positive or negative) you hold about your post-trauma self. For each one, identify how that shows some good and wholesome quality about you that is valued in the world outside trauma.

~~~~~

Beneath the junk of trauma is the pure essence of who you are.

Regardless of what you have survived, you are still human. This means you retain some purely human traits that, although the mask of trauma may be hiding them right now, continue to exist.

In your humanity lie the seeds of your pure essence. For example, consider your ability to:

- feel **love** (even if it's just the sound of the rain on the roof)

- experience **compassion** (even if it's just for a small animal)

- encounter **joy** (even if it's just in the first notes of a favorite song)

- notice **desire** (even if it's just for a good, long nap)

These facets of yourself are immutable. You will always have the capacity, among other things, to love, laugh, and feel some measure of joy and happiness. These are all part of your human genetic code as much as sadness, grief, fear, and anger.

You carry these positive elements of who you are with you. In every moment the opportunity exists to excavate and experience them.

> Choose one of the elements in the preceding list. Imagine your life as a timeline, the past stretching out in a straight line. Walk back into it, looking for the times over your life when you have experienced that pure essence. Then bring yourself back to the present moment. Peer out into the future and design a moment for yourself to explore embodying this element again.

~~~~~

Your perception of experience directly affects your personal identity.

What you think about and the meaning you give what you experience creates your vision of reality.

Your perspective of the world is unique to you as an individual and makes you who you are.

You are a person who feels...and believes...and wants...and sees...and interprets...as...

In this way, perception plays a key role during trauma, which means it also plays a key role afterward.

> Consider how you see yourself. Make a list of five negative aspects that define you. Then make a list of five positive things that define you. Your default mode is going to be the negative. Spend the rest of the day seeing how often you can choose, act, think, and behave from the positive side of the list.

~~~~~

You cannot change the past or your traumatic experience, but you can change the future and how you function in it.

Many survivors want to go back to "who I used to be," or regret never having had the chance to be someone unaffected by trauma.

Survivors often lose many years trying to go back, only to discover the truth: You can only go forward.

The key to going forward lies in finding new ways to be who you are that are unrelated to the horror in your past.

If you were going to describe yourself as if your trauma never happened, what would that sound like?

Hint: Even if your trauma began at birth, this exercise applies to you; it has more to do with how you *would like to imagine* yourself than who you were on track to becoming before trauma occurred.

P.S. This is a tough exercise. Start by setting the intention (see page 107) to mull this over and discover the answer over a period of time.

~~~~~

Be brave enough to see the truth of who you are.

You are a magnificent, whole human being. The exploration of that truth starts with three specific questions:

1. *Who were you before your trauma?* Before life experiences occurred, you were a blank slate. Looking back means remembering the innocence into which you were born, plus who you used to be or who you imagine you could have been prior to trauma.

In your notebook, journal, or computer, take a few moments to jot down a brief description of your past self, remembered or imagined.

2. *Who have you become since your trauma?* Specifically identifying how trauma has affected you begins the process of recognizing (a) the changes you value and wish to keep (since there are positive aspects of post-trauma change), and (b) the post-trauma alterations you'd like to revise or release.

Take a few moments to jot down how trauma has changed you, both positively and negatively.

3. *Who do you want to be now?* It's probably been a long time since you thought you had choices about who you are, which means it may have been a long time since you allowed yourself to daydream about who that would be. Start compiling a wish list.

Take a few moments to jot down ideas for who you would like to be.

> **Note:** *The answers to these three questions remain constantly dynamic. They will shift and change as you shift and change.*

~~~~~

Be a hero.

According to the dictionary, *hero* means a person of "distinguished courage and ability."

Right off the bat, how much do you think that definition applies to you? While you struggle with PTSD, it may seem strange to see yourself as heroic. But you absolutely have a heroic self because you:

- survived something horrific
- continue to live despite the pain
- struggle to cope, reclaim, and rebuild
- seek the path to freedom

Only heroes do all of those things.

The crux of recovery comes from shifting from powerless to powerful. Accessing your heroic self is a great way to do that.

> Take out a pen and piece of paper and write, "I am a hero," ten times. Pause; how does that feel? Write it another ten times. Pause again. Repeat this process until you've written the phrase

a hundred times. What would it take for you to fully accept
yourself as someone who is courageous and able?

~~~~~

Your identity is the fact of being you.

(Re)claiming a wholesome sense of safety and control is a central theme
of trauma recovery. If you want to feel this way at work, at home, in the
street, in the world, in relationships, or anywhere else, there's only one thing
constant in any scenario: you.

The term *identity* relates to the conceptual idea of who you are, how you
describe yourself according to what makes you unique, plus what defines you
and your place as a person in the world. This self-definition makes you feel
good or horrible about yourself: It's what makes you feel that you have what
it takes to heal or that you will live a long and horrible post-traumatic life.

If you feel changed or diminished by trauma, then you are experiencing
a common post-trauma identity crisis: You used to be one person (or prior
to trauma you had the opportunity to become someone) and now you're
someone else. Who are you now? And what the heck are you supposed to do
about who you will become? These are confusing and tough questions that
healing will answer.

Take a stab at one of the other definitions today. The more you
consider, alter, try out, and expand your self-definition, the more
you will grow and change. Use any of the following prompts:

- I would define myself as…

- My friend(s) would describe me as…

- Who I want to be is…

- My objective is to become…

- In the future I hope to be…

THE ROLE OF IDENTITY IN PTSD RECOVERY

You, and only you, choose and define who you are.

Identity refers to how you describe yourself, which depends on the specific characteristics you choose to highlight as making you the unique person that you are. True, trauma has changed your identity insofar as it affects your self-description—but your identity (like your body and all of its systems) is designed to constantly change, which means it's poised to change again right this minute.

In the spirit of continued identity formation, your only choice now is to push your identity development by going forward. You need to make new choices about the person you wish to be and create a post-trauma self that restores and combines all of the best of who you were before (even if you can't fully remember or know) and who you had the potential to be (if trauma occurred before you had the chance for any self-expression) with the best of who you are today and the vision of who you wish to become in the future.

Although the process may feel uncomfortable, the forward-only prescription works to your benefit. Consider this: Who you are is a function of what you decide. It has zero to do with what you have experienced.

Who would you choose to be? Answer that question in your notebook, journal, or computer now:

If I could choose to be any kind of person, I would choose to be...

You develop your identity by making (or not making) various choices about what you think about who you are and what you have experienced.

Taking back the power trauma steals from you begins with taking back your power to name yourself—not as a survivor, but as something else. It means taking back the power to see yourself not as a victim, but as someone more positive and empowered (even if that feels uncomfortable at first) who now has a future to engage in and enjoy.

The key to developing your post-trauma identity lies in being very deliberate in perceiving the person you wish to be. It's easy to see the negative elements of yourself but much harder to recognize, embrace, and embody the positive. And yet, those good elements are the ones that most purely define who you are, can, and could be!

Start developing a thought process in which you consciously take these steps:

- Imagine yourself without trauma: Who might you have been without your traumatic experience?

- Imagine yourself without PTSD: What could you be doing if PTSD didn't get in the way?

- Identify traits and characteristics you would like to possess: What kinds of qualities would you like to develop when trauma and PTSD obstacles are removed?

- Identify and plan objectives to move you forward: What activities can you engage in that will evolve you toward the person you would like to be?

To reclaim a positive and whole sense of self, look for similarities both in the past and in the present.

There are many puzzle pieces in the philosophy of identity, but two theories will be useful in how you think about yourself:

- *Synchronic identity* is an attempt to explain what characterizes an entity at a given time (and makes it identical to another in the same circumstance). Ask yourself, "What traits, qualities, and features define who I am in any single moment?"

- *Diachronic identity* is an attempt to explain what makes an entity at one time identical to an entity existing at another time. Ask yourself, "What defines who I am over a period of time?"

While trauma has rocked the solid foundation of who you are, the truth is that both synchronic and diachronic elements of your identity are still available to you. They will be the building blocks of your post-trauma identity.

Pause throughout the day and ask yourself the preceding questions. Mull over the ideas and capture the answers in your notebook, journal, or computer, where you can see the full picture that emerges.

Restoring your identity leads to a grounded sense of safety.

While your identity develops throughout your lifetime, the main work of its original formation usually occurs during adolescence (thirteen to eighteen years of age) when you develop your individuality and form the norms, beliefs, rituals, values, desires, and practices that guide how you interact with your environment. This process is, in fact, considered the key developmental task of adolescence.

If you were traumatized prior to or during this time, it makes sense that the distortions of post-trauma life could have impeded your ability to form an identity outside the trauma realm. This means you're not really the person you could have been, or would have chosen to be, if trauma had been absent.

Regardless of when your trauma occurred, however, the road to restoring your identity begins with becoming aware of its components and actively (re) engaging them. The major developmental aspect of identity is considered completed when you construct a satisfying plan about your future.

After trauma, and especially in the presence of PTSD, it can be incredibly difficult or even impossible to imagine any future at all. This is another reason why restoring your identity can be so critical to recovery: It gives you a vision for a continued life long after trauma's interruption.

> Pretend that tomorrow you will wake up and your recovery will miraculously be complete. Freed from your PTSD prison, what experiences would you hope to have over the course of the next year?

~~~~

Identity is a kaleidoscope whose beauty emerges from the ever-changing mix of colorful pieces that constantly arrange and rearrange as you yourself turn the tube.

You have a great power within you. When your life was threatened, you used this power to survive. (This is true even if you froze during the event.) Now this power to survive resides in your mind, heart, body, and soul. It is a part of you and courses through you the same way your blood is a part of you and courses through you.

In every moment, you have the choice to act from this place of power. In every moment, you create who you are through each decision you make and action you take. It's okay to have days when your kaleidoscope fills with darkened pieces of glass. In those moments, remember that the power you contain means you can always shift the kaleidoscope to let in more light and rearrange the pieces.

Darken your kaleidoscope: Identify five things about yourself that bother, upset, or disturb you.

Now lighten it: For each item identified, name the strength, power, or positive element that it represents.

~~~~

Reclaim control by making choices and taking actions based on what you want today, versus the trauma that makes you feel you need to be able to bury your fear of what happened yesterday.

If you are a survivor of childhood trauma, you probably became so altered by those experiences that you never had the chance to become the person you could have been if you'd had the opportunity to grow up in a world that felt safe. Like a tree forced to grow in a crooked direction, you never had the chance to grow straight up toward the sun. Similarly, if you were older at the time of your trauma, you may notice that you were originally solid and stable in your self-definition but now question how the effects of trauma have morphed you into someone new—a tree that used to grow straight up toward the sun, but today leans crookedly.

Up until now, trauma has been calling the shots. Coping in that place takes a lot of energy and focus. While you've been busy developing and maintaining this new lifestyle, you may have avoided recognizing the You it has created. Acknowledging this new self is an important step toward reclaiming your self-definition.

Finish this prompt by choosing a metaphor (image, analogy, or comparison) or simile (a description using *like* or *as*) for how trauma has changed you:

Since my trauma, I am (like)...

What are the pros and cons of being this?

Take stock of your identity inventory.

Every merchandise store has days set aside for inventory assessment. The purpose is for the staff to be aware of what's on the shelf at that moment, which products move, which ones don't, what needs to be ordered and when. Inventory assessments keep the store balanced and appropriately stocked.

Your post-trauma identity is like a grocery store that's constantly receiving a high volume of traffic. Being aware of what's on the shelves of who you are—and whether the items are desirable or need to be replaced—allows you to constantly interact with your continued development.

Once a month, do your own inventory. Take your first one today:

- Identify elements of yourself that you appreciate in the present moment. Think of how you speak, dress, work, act, behave, interact with others, present yourself in the world, rest, play, learn, develop, think, and feel. Share this appreciation with someone you trust by explaining what you appreciate and why it's important to you. Develop a plan to maintain, or even expand, these elements.

- Notice what aspects of yourself have passed their expiration dates. Imagine you can clear them off the shelf of who you are. What would have to happen in order for them to be removed? How can you start doing that? Who can help?

Your post-trauma self, built on a sense of positive inner connection and an "I can handle it!" attitude, already exists; your job now is to discover it.

Your self-definition is the beginning of what makes you hope, believe, and work toward healing. Developing a healthy post-trauma identity (one in which you revise your vision of yourself as victim or outcast, and come to perceive yourself as a competent, creative, adaptive, self-reliant, protective, and skilled individual) can catapult recovery to a new level and inject it with incredible momentum by grounding you within yourself.

Trauma kicked you out of the self you knew or wished you had a chance to become. Creating your post-trauma identity is the act of hauling yourself back into yourself with force, determination, and commitment.

To develop a solid post-trauma identity, you must see yourself beyond the facts and effects of trauma.

Start identifying your post-trauma identity by mulling over this question:

How would you like to define yourself when your recovery is complete?

The answer to this question, more than any other, forms the backbone of a recovery focus that can deliver you out of the darkness of who you are today into the light of who you're wishing so much to be tomorrow.

There is a part of you that knows it's time to evolve and change and is seeking ways to do that.

Regardless of and despite your past, you can create your present and future; this is a technical fact. Philosophically, you have free will. Psychologically, you have resilience. Scientifically, you regenerate. Although today you may feel moments of hopelessness, that is just a *feeling* created by a *thought* that produces a *chemical release* in your body.

When you feel unhappy, uncomfortable, or disturbed, pause for a moment. Then ask yourself, "What thought did I have just before this feeling occurred?" If you can't identify the thought, ask, "What did I just hear, see, taste, smell, or touch just before this feeling occurred?" Recognizing the thought (or the experience that created a thought/memory) helps you be present, connect to your executive thinking self, and develop your feeling of strength and connection. It also allows you to separate who you are from your response to a thought or experience. The more you make this separation, the more you open space for the part of you that desires change to enter your healing process.

Be very quiet and still; close your eyes if that feels comfortable.

Imagine that the part of you who knows and is ready to create change enters the room and sits beside you.

What knowledge does this person have that will allow you to feel on track, connected, and focused during your recovery process?

Ask for guidance; listen to the answers and incorporate them into your healing.

~~~~~

You are the past and the present combined.

Too often we ignore, avoid, or are told to release what we've lost, but that's not always what creates healing. Sometimes, there's a reason to hold on and to find a way to use what you're holding onto in positive and healthy ways.

Feeling better comes from clarifying, identifying, reclaiming, restoring, embodying, embracing, and exhibiting those aspects of who you are, have been, or wish to be that are meaningful to you. By looking back, you acknowledge and validate the truth of the person you used to be, or might have been, without the interruption of trauma. You connect with the goodness in that person and learn to infuse those strengths into who you are today.

In exercising the power to access past elements, you begin constructing a post-trauma identity that resonates with and fits you. While you can discard any disconnected past qualities that did not suit you, at the same time you can deliberately choose to bring forward those that you miss, value, love, and wish to have again.

What did you most value about your pre-trauma self or the
possibility of that self? Name three things. Choose one that,
for the next week, you will intentionally embody and express at
least three times per day.

~~~

Shift from "if only" to "and now" thinking.

Speaking on my radio show, trauma and PTSD expert Dr. Rachel Yehuda
remarked, "We don't have eyes in the back of our heads for a reason." She was
expressing the idea that we're not supposed to spend our lives looking behind.

Yet, when you are stuck in PTSD, that's exactly what you so often do. One
aspect of this particularly influences how you perceive the past in relation
to your present.

It's normal to think, "If only trauma hadn't happened I could..."

Any disappointment, missed opportunities, and lack of personal or
professional success can be attributed to what could have happened if
trauma hadn't.

There's a time and place for that kind of thought as you grieve the losses
that trauma causes. However, if you want to heal, you're going to have to
stop telling your trauma story. You and your opportunities are so much more
than your "if only" limitations.

To be able to heal, you're going to have to start telling a new story based
on what can, might, or could happen starting today and going forward.

Start training your brain to look ahead rather than behind. Play
the "and now" game with yourself today: For every loss thought,
follow it with "And now I will/can/want..."

~~~

Deep and meaningful change will happen when you decide it's time.

PTSD symptoms and other elements distract you from your true essence. However, with change being the rule rather than the exception, you have the opportunity to rewrite, reconceive, and reconstruct yourself in any moment.

Training your brain to shift attention where you choose to place it is an important scientific element of PTSD recovery. When you construct your post-trauma identity (a vision of yourself beyond trauma), you're doing for yourself psychologically what brain training does for you physically: You make a deliberate shift from seeing yourself one way to seeing yourself in another, healthier way.

While PTSD symptoms can make it seem as though you have little ability to define yourself outside the effects of trauma, how you perceive yourself is *always* an element of choice that hinges on your willingness to change.

Are you ready to expand beyond your victim/survivor identity? Mull over this question and then spend some time finishing this sentence with pen and paper:

I am ready to redefine who I am because...

Defining who you are finds its foundation in "I am" statements.

At their best, "I am" statements are simple sentences that pair your own recognition of yourself with what you want; at their worst, they pair who you are with what you don't want. Consider these examples:

I am strong and courageous.

vs.

I am a powerless victim.

Normally, you probably don't walk around being conscious of the negative "I am" statements that swirl through your head. They don't light up with the usual "danger" neon sign, so it's easy to overlook them in favor of the threats you can actually see, hear, and feel. But what if every negative

"I am" statement did light up and flash? Starting this moment, let's say that they do. Now you're going to begin raising your awareness of them, as well as deliberately crafting the "I am" statements by which you wish to live.

- **Step One: Make a list of ten positive "I am" statements.** Begin with statements that are true today. Start with something simple, for example, "I am hopeful." Spend some time thinking about what defines you in this moment that is unimpeachable and good. When you have completed this, go deeper, to more complex definitions, and add ten more. (Use the earlier diachronic and synchronic questions from page 141 for added perspective.)

- **Step Two: Make a list of the qualities you admire about your past self or the person you could have been.** Choose the top five that mean the most to you. Craft "I am" statements using these details. How do these statements feel? What would it take to make them feel like comfortable, accurate representations of who you are today? How can you embody/express each statement in daily life?

- **Step Three: Make a list of qualities that you like about yourself today.** Choose the top five that mean the most to you. Craft "I am" statements using these details. How can you exhibit each of these qualities more thoroughly and with more intention?

As you move through this exercise, resist the urge to worry if developing your "I am" statements feels phony or inappropriate. If you don't fully connect with or exhibit them immediately, that's okay. Sometimes you have to introduce an idea and warm up to it. This is part of the process of accepting and inhabiting it. Expect to encounter this kind of challenge, and allow yourself to move through it. If it feels more comfortable, amend your statement to "I am open to being...."

You create your world, your life, and your experiences based on what you believe.

What you say to yourself about yourself is what you will see, hear, feel, and experience.

What you believe about yourself is what you bring to you, both by the experiences you seek or don't seek, and the experiences that others choose for you, based on their perceptions of the persona you inhabit.

At first, as you explore the process of creating positive self-definition statements, using the word *I* may feel uncomfortable. When you're disconnected from your inner self, the word *I* can seem not to have an internal referent. This means there is no *I* below the surface of how you show up in the world and get through the day.

As happens often in trauma recovery, what you feel is different from what is true. *I* does exist for you; it's just a matter of reconnecting and getting used to it, plus learning to parlay a thought, feeling, or desire into a statement that refers to who you are in a way that feels acceptable to you.

In their purest essence, "I am" statements are all about standing up for and choosing who you are, but first you can do that from a third-person perspective. Imagine what kinds of statements you want to define you. Then, in your notebook, journal, or computer, craft some statements that reflect that about someone else; for example, "She is a good person who follows her heart and, in every moment, tries to do what's best for herself and others."

~~~~~~

A major anchor for identity is the sense of connection you feel to meaningful elements throughout your lifetime.

For example, consider your love of animals, your ability to be compassionate, or how you feel when you engage in an activity you love.

Trauma provokes emotional and physical reactions that cause a break in the linkage between you and your familiar elements. This leads to a fracture in the overall structure of your inner world. Consequently, you may feel as if something important has been lost or is unavailable, and that the balance of the person you thought you were or could have been tips in a new and uncomfortable direction.

Reclaiming a sense of connection can be found through any of the following elements:

- specifically creating new experiences

- developing an idea of a normal future

- purposely embodying a positive aspect of your self

- identifying and aligning with personality traits you admire

- spending time with others you enjoy and trust

- restricting the context in which you perceive yourself

- venturing out into the world in small ways

- rewriting the narrative of your trauma

- feeling good and powerful in your body

- restoring (or adding new) meaningful values

Choose any one of the preceding elements and brainstorm what you can do to form a connection to yourself through that option.

~~~~~~

Knowing (and even more importantly, liking) your identity is like putting gas in a car: It gives you fuel to move.

Feelings of grief and anger over the impact of trauma deplete a core source of your strength. Harboring a slew of deep, powerful negative ideas, feelings, and energy about yourself drains your energy and makes forward motion all but impossible.

Louise Hay, author of many bestselling books and founder of Hay House Publishing, once said that, after her thirty-plus years studying the best techniques for self-improvement, she's distilled them all down to one action: Learn to love yourself.

While loving your whole self during recovery is often a difficult task, there are things about you to be loved and admired. Make a list of twenty lovable/admirable things about you. If you have trouble filling up the list, ask people you trust for their input.

ACTIVATING YOUR SELF-DEFINITION PROCESS

Access your best self.

In psychological terms, an *identity crisis* is "a period of uncertainty and confusion in which a person's sense of identity becomes insecure, typically due to a change in their expected aims or role in society," (Oxford Dictionaries). Isn't that exactly what happens after trauma?

The ensuing identity loss can shift you into enormous self-doubt, feeding the frenzy of the post-trauma physiological responses and further disempowering you as you (consciously or unconsciously) struggle to determine: Who are you now? Are you defined by your past, present, or future?

Reduce the confusion by stabilizing the chaos: Resolve the identity crisis by deliberately developing a self-definition that gives you boundaries, perspective, inspiration, motivation, and direction that place you in alignment with what feels good, natural, and right. In the post-trauma world, those feelings are the highest currency, because they give you the energy to engage in recovery and succeed.

In your notebook, journal, or computer, enter one quality you admire about who you are. That can be the way you treat others, your work ethic, your commitment to family, some act you have performed, or even how you continue to get out of bed in the morning despite the PTSD fog and weight.

Now challenge yourself to intentionally make use of that quality five times over the course of the next twenty-four hours.

Self-definition helps you gain clarity about yourself, your choices, and what your future can be.

When you think about answering the question, "Who am I now?" a useful guide includes two key factors:

- **Values are things upon which you place great importance.** They are the principles by which you live your life and the standard to which you hold your own and others' behaviors. Being clear on your values (qualities and experiences that are important to you) is like having a road map for living; it tells you when to turn and which road to go down to get to the desired destination.

- **Desires are critical in your post-trauma world.** Getting back in touch with what you want puts you in touch with a life-affirming energy. It also puts you in touch with your desire to live. Asking yourself, "What do I want?" in any moment—and focusing on healthy answers to that question—then giving those things to yourself puts you in the process of beginning to create the experiences and life you most wish to have.

Start identifying your values and desires. Crease a piece of paper into two columns; label them "Values" and "Desires." Then write out as many values and desires you can think of. When you've exhausted your ideas, put the page down and return to it at a later time to continue.

~~~~~

Reclaiming control requires you to respond versus react, create versus accept.

All of this begins with your vision. Your thoughts create your reality. You live, experience, and feel what you *think*. This means what you think (and how you represent it to yourself through the voice in your head, the interpretations you assign, and the pictures you make in your mind) is the number-one most critical element in coping and eventually healing PTSD.

Where you focus your attention and what pictures you make in your mind work in a feedback loop of thought and feeling creation. This is exactly the origin of your control. By developing daily practices that strengthen your ability to decide what pictures you allow your mind to create, you take back a little bit more control, moment by moment.

> Notice when you have a bad feeling. Pause and imagine there's a movie screen in your mind. What picture(s) does the thought project on the screen? Let the picture fade to black. Then lighten the empty screen and deliberately project a new picture—one that reflects a kind/happy/hopeful/supportive/feel-good image.

~~~~~

You and your life are measured by the sum of all things.

Gaining perspective means seeing things from a 360-degree view. This encompasses four important vantage points:

1. The arc of your whole life, from the day you were born until your last breath

2. The arc of the simple moment you're in: from zero to sixty seconds

3. The negative aspects of what you have experienced in either arc

4. The positive events that have made a difference in either arc

Who you are is an ever-evolving compilation of these elements and their many individual facets.

> Answer the following four questions to begin exploring yourself in these areas:

1. Describe in writing who you are (so far) from what you
   know about you from birth until today.

2. Set a timer for sixty seconds. During that single minute,
   sit and be present with yourself. Suspend judgment. Then
   describe who you are based on what you notice about
   yourself in those sixty seconds.

3. Describe who you are due to the negative events you
   have experienced.

4. Describe who you are due to the positive events you
   have experienced.

5. And now for the real challenge: Set your PTSD symptoms
   aside. Define yourself according to everything else
   about you.

~~~~~

You are one personality, but many selves.

As a zygote (a newly fertilized egg), you began with a whole, pure,
untraumatized self. Then life happened. In response to experiences, different
selves developed. This is normal for everyone, regardless of trauma.

The difference with trauma is that it causes fragmentation of the coherent
self: Rather than working together as one unit, selves exist in a state of frantic
chaos with confrontational agendas.

Now, within your overall single personality, these selves represent
conflicting internal states, desires, and beliefs that affect your daily thoughts,
feelings, and behaviors.

Reflect on what it feels like inside yourself. How do you
experience the presence of different parts? In your notebook,

journal, or computer, enter some of the parts/selves you notice operating on a consistent basis.

~~~~~

The purpose of your parts is to allow you to do, be, think, feel, act, and behave according to your choices.

You contain parts for every behavior. For example, if you choose to indulge anger, there's a part of you that knows how to do that very well. On the other hand, if you choose to be mindfully aware of when anger is coming on and take an action to divert it, there's a part of you that knows (or can learn) how to do that, too.

A significant mission in recovery is deciding which part(s) or self (selves) you want to have the most power in your daily life. Then you can make choices and take actions that give it that power to direct and redirect the course of your day.

The more choices you make, the more actions you take, and the more strongly you craft who you are, the more you decide which self is ultimately in control and the more you succeed in healing.

Begin building a newly whole self.

Part One:

- Identify and list your most dominant parts (e.g., your warrior self, addictive self, sad self, I-want-to-give-up self, hopeful self).

- Individually acknowledge what each one needs/wants.

- Make a plan for how they can work together to achieve their objectives.

Part Two:

- Identify five negative parts of yourself and then five positive parts of who you are.

- Write down what choices and actions need to be made and taken for you to live more from the five positive parts and less from the negative parts.

~~~~

Give a proper good-bye to the old you.

In a perfect world, when you depart from a close friend, you take the time to create the opportunity to exchange some meaningful words, and perhaps even clasp for a good long hug.

One of the problems with trauma is that things happen so fast. There is no time for good-bye as a part of you is ripped away and severed from your daily existence.

Through traumatic events out of your control, you instantly lost a part(s) of yourself or your chance(s) to be someone that you liked. That's so absolutely unfair.

The grief and sadness (even anger) that come from this abrupt separation can fuel PTSD symptoms. Or you can soothe the burn by acknowledging the old you, validating how you feel about her and why, and giving her a meaningful sendoff.

Write a letter to your past self or who you could have been. Tell that self everything you love about her and why she still remains meaningful to you. Then say whatever you think she would like to hear to soothe the disconnection that happened much too quickly.

(Of course, this part will always be with you. The process suggested here is one that actually reunites you in a way that feels comfortable and connected.)

~~~~~

Reintegrating the fragmented parts adds power, confidence, calm, and self-mastery to your healing process.

PTSD recovery is tough enough without your interior self feeling disjointed and out of control, which is exactly why addressing the identity crisis at the core of trauma can be so useful in recovery. Pulling yourself back into one solid entity—constructing a post-trauma identity—that works in concert with itself brings all of your energy into a central, accessible location. From there, you can make substantial choices and take meaningful and successful actions that move you forward in recovery.

To begin, use any of these post-trauma identity actions to infuse your recovery with more clarity, opportunity, and success.

- Get in touch with parts of yourself that you admire (even though you may doubt their existence, they are present); identify, name, and choose how to act from their perspective.

- Use your non-trauma-related skills and traits for added strength in healing.

- Develop a self-definition in which the fact of your trauma becomes a small part of the larger concept of who you are.

- Define yourself and your life first by the affirmative, powerful, supportive, reliable, and feel-good elements (look for them, they are there) of who you are.

- (Re)connect to a positive and empowered sense of successfully achieving tasks, objectives, and actions.

- Create a vision for the Future You that feels productive, meaningful, and prepared to handle life.

- Use healthy choices and actions to expand the way you, others, and the world perceive you.

- Teach your fragmented selves to work as a team.

- Strengthen your recovery focus by having a clear healing intention (see page 114 for how to create an active intention).

~~~~~

Honor, respect, and work with your past selves.

Without a doubt, trauma changes you. It teaches you things about yourself, others, and the world that challenge beliefs and alter how you interact. Since your trauma, you may notice that you feel you are different from who you were before the event—even if that event was birth. You may feel you have lost access to important parts of yourself, or lost qualities or characteristics that were important to you. If your trauma occurred before you had a chance to form an identity, you may feel that trauma prevented you from becoming the person you wish you had had a chance to be. While all of that *feels* true...it's a myth.

Here's the real truth: If you can remember or imagine an alternative self, then that self already exists in you.

Right now you have the option of engaging any self that seems relevant to healing. Is it the four-year-old, the twenty-year-old, your compassionate self, your intentional self, or your [*fill in the blank*] self that you really wish would step in and help out right now?

If you'd like connection to that part, all you have to do is ask...

Identify the part of you that seems like she would add the most benefit to your process today. Then find ways to connect with her: Invite her to participate in your recovery effort; spend time with her in some fun activity; let her spirit, energy, and advice infuse you with a sense of connection, direction, and stimulation.

~~~

Regardless of the trauma(s) you survived, your Core Self remains constant, like an eternal flame.

When you live from your core, you live from your true self—the Real You, which is always available and is held within your identity the way your heart is held within your body. At any time, you can choose to liberate elements of this part of who you are to both deepen your identity connection and lead you forward in genuine movement.

Think of identity as having three levels:

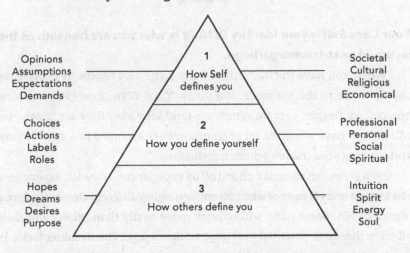

Opinions
Assumptions
Expectations
Demands

1 How Self defines you

Societal
Cultural
Religious
Economical

Choices
Actions
Labels
Roles

2 How you define yourself

Professional
Personal
Social
Spiritual

Hopes
Dreams
Desires
Purpose

3 How others define you

Intuition
Spirit
Energy
Soul

- **Level 3** is how you're partially defined from the outside and comes from your interactions in the world. On this level you present yourself to the world, and definitions occur based on how you're perceived by the people around you.

- **Level 2** is how you're partially defined from inside your head, based on your thoughts. Here, you create your conscious vision of yourself through posturing to be known in a certain way.

- **Level 1** is how you're wholly defined by the deeply internal feelings of your authentic Core Self. At this level there are no outside or inside influences; there is just the true You allowing itself to be known.

Clear some time to sit quietly, closing your eyes if that feels comfortable. Imagine your Core Self visits you and the two of you have a chance to chat. Ask for guidance about how to connect with, embody, and behave from this part of you.

Your Core Self is your identity DNA; it is who you are beneath all the layers of post-trauma garbage.

When you have the flu, various body parts and functions experience changes due to the presence of a virus. Your DNA, however, remains unchanged. Despite your flu symptoms (and long after they are gone), you will always have a specific set of chromosomes arranged in a specific way and carrying your unique genetic information.

Your genes can be turned on and off by experiences. Likewise, experiences can turn on and off parts of who you are, activating different elements of your identity DNA. Some parts will activate more easily than others, but they all have the same potential to engage or disengage. The deciding factor is your ongoing experience, which you can create through focus, dedication, and action.

Do you see yourself predominantly as a survivor, someone who has been victimized, can't get justice, and will always be damaged by the past? Having this mindset is like jumping into Lake Michigan in January and then lounging on the beach: You're just asking for pneumonia. In this scenario, every moment will appear threatening and energy-sapping, and the identity DNA you activate will increase your stress and continue to bring you victimizing experiences.

However, every element of identity is constantly mutable, which means the present moment—and its details—can all be changed.

Get out of the cold and take yourself to a Caribbean island: Pull your chair into the heat of the equatorial sun and let the warmth revive your spirit. Balance your negative, threat-seeking self by allowing its opposite to occasionally appear: Approach the world as if people are waiting to help, support, and love you.

Imagine this: PTSD is a virus to which your mind and body must mount a defense. When the virus has been overcome, your core identity DNA will once again emerge as the authentic you. The fever of your soul will dissipate, your appetite for life will return, and slowly you'll regain your strength to engage in new experiences and adventures.

You cannot go back to who you used to be.

It's natural after trauma—when the world suddenly seems unrecognizable—to immediately look for what seems familiar. One way to do this is to seek what you remember is familiar about you and then try to go back there. Or, if your trauma occurred at a very young age, your impulse might be to focus on what you wish you'd had a chance to have, be, or do. In either scenario, this process only causes heartache. As you have probably already discovered, you can't go back. You can imitate that old self or mourn lost opportunities, but you can never be that old self again or revise your history. Right now, stop trying.

Instead, flip your point of view: That old self, real or imagined, lives on in a parallel reality. You are in a new reality and must make your own way.

Rather than reject who you are today in favor of that other self, make her proud of you.

> Think of the person you used to be or wish you'd had a chance to become. What can you do today that would make her proud of and respect who you are?

~~~~~

A very strong part of you wants you to heal.

A main factor in how you define yourself is the context in which you understand where and how you belong. Since your trauma(s), your identity has changed, because your understanding of who you are and the world in which you live has dramatically altered.

Losing a sense of safety, control, and certainty shifts you into a *less-than* feeling. Perhaps today you see yourself as someone robbed of innocence, trust, love, well-being, and a feeling of being able to protect yourself. You may imagine, and even deeply feel, that you are damaged, emotionally or psychologically disfigured, or undesirable. This new self-definition affects how you see the world, think about yourself and others, and make choices and take actions.

Although your new identity seems bleak, another part of you sees the bigger picture. That's the part that inspires and motivates you to move toward reclaiming a more positive, solid, stable, and proactive sense of self. While your *less-than* self may hold control over who you are today, your *more-than* self gains ground in every moment you work toward restoring yourself. It is your *more-than* self that forms the basis of who you will become when you (re)construct your identity.

> Your *more-than* self wants many good, positive, and healthy things for you. Get in touch with her today. Invite her to sit beside you and make a list of all the things she wants for you.

In different moments and situations, different selves rise up to take control.

When you're struggling after trauma, there are moments when you feel strong, and others in which you feel weak; days when you have clarity, and others that feel as if you move through a fog. You probably cycle through those experiences very aware of how different selves seem to leap into action without any organization and often without your consent. For example, you know that when you feel doubt, sometimes, out of nowhere "that other self" steps forth with faith and belief. Or, you want to experience courage, but just when you try to access it, another self steps forward, full of fear.

How you ultimately decide which self is in control (and when) comes from deliberate choices, actions, and a clear definition of which self/selves you want to engage in daily life.

In your notebook, journal, or computer, name the self that most often takes control of how you think, feel, and behave.

Is this the self who will help you heal so that you transform into a strong, confident, and capable person?

Which self would you rather see calling the shots? What are the benefits of this self being in control?

How can you access, connect to, and invite that self to emerge more often?

The more choices you make, the more strongly you craft who you are, the more you decide which self is the one most in control.

How do you do this? You'll find ways that suit your particular personality and situation. In the meantime, test these ideas:

- **Understand what drives your dominant selves.** Name the dominant selves you identified on page 157. Now identify and describe the *purpose* or *mission* of each one.

- **Identify which important qualities each self possesses.** Becoming clear on what each self offers helps you know which self to call upon and in which circumstances.

- **Talk to each of the selves you identify.** Ask what they want for you and how they can help you achieve that.

- **Write a letter to each self.** Describe how you want them to give the help they have to offer, and when, and in what way, specifically.

- **Practice accessing each self.** In moments that don't matter, allow each of the selves you most want to experience to take over control; allow them to stay in control for as long as possible.

> For a while, this process may seem strange, as if you're playing a silly game. That's okay. The more familiar you become with who those selves are and how you can access them, the more you become consciously familiar with who you are, in your entirety. The more you do that and the more you become present, the more opportunities you will have to step forward into your chosen self and the life you most deeply desire.

~~~~~

Who are you now? You are the person you choose to be.

If your identity were a company, it would be about to experience a massive overhaul of personnel and departmental reorganization. In restructuring your identity after trauma, you collapse the fragmented self and worldview that trauma put in place; from the rubble, you construct a new orientation that promotes wholeness, plus a perspective based on a mission and vision designed to support the success of your desired life.

What, or who, is at the core of the being that is you?

Spend some time meditating on or daydreaming or journaling about what self you imagine is at the very center of your heart. Describe that person.

As long as your heart beats, that person remains a substantial part of you. Identify three elements that you feel have, can, and will remain true about you no matter what.

Why are these elements important to you?

How can you embody these elements through your choices and actions today?

Constructing your post-trauma identity will affect who you are all the way down to a cellular level.

How you see yourself (and how that makes you feel about yourself) plays a huge role in both your body and mind. When you change the perceptions you hold about yourself and the meanings you ascribe to who you are, you change your body chemistry, which in turn changes your mind. The feedback loop and its benefits are endless.

Remember: A thought produces a physical reaction. Literally, every thought you have (positive or negative, powerful or powerless) creates chemical releases in your brain that create reflective sensations (feelings) in your body (along with other alterations in physical processing). When you diligently put in place a plan (and stick to it) for creating an identity that feels good to you—and optimizing how you interact with your body and mind—you will find yourself feeling, thinking, and behaving differently. Strengthening this process begins with giving yourself permission.

Right now, give yourself permission by writing yourself a letter that begins, "*[fill in your name here]*, I give you permission to..."

~~~~~~

Throughlines connect the past to the present.

In books, movies, and plays, a "throughline" is a connecting theme that runs from the beginning to the end of the plot. It's a consistency in the objective(s) of a character. Rocky, for example, remains committed to becoming a boxing champ. He loves boxing in the beginning of the film and soars to its heights by the end.

"What is my trauma throughline?" might not be a question you're asking yourself, but it can be an instrumental question to answer in post-trauma recovery—especially if you're seeking your post-trauma identity. Who are you now? Definitely, you're different than who you were before trauma, but is anything the same?

Sometimes, it can help to look back at who you used to be in order to discover some clues. This is true whether you have a clear before/after break, or even if you were traumatized at birth and don't have a direct sense of who you "used to be."

No matter what your trauma has been or when it happened, there are positive throughlines in who you are, what you love, and what you do. To discover them, think back over your past and ask yourself:

- What have I always loved?
- What's my favorite memory?
- What was my favorite activity as a child?
- What has always made me laugh?
- What has always made me feel a sense of belonging?
- What have I always wished for?
- What have I always wanted?
- What experience have I always enjoyed?

How can you create experiences of some or all of these things in your life today?

Inventing the new you = Curiosity + Adventure + Willing Uncertainty

Like the rest of recovery, becoming your Future Self is a process that requires successive steps taken slowly over a period of time. You will be translating thoughts, feelings, and ideas into concrete evidence in the physical world. If that sounds challenging, think of yourself as an inventor:

You conceptualize and sketch out the gadget; then you build the physical prototype.

Many of the previous concepts in this book have introduced you to methods for conceiving and developing aspects of the New You. Implementing visualization and solidifying processes to bring that self closer on a daily basis will begin your transition into embodying elements and aspects of the self you wish to engage.

Ultimately, that self will feel so close that you easily step into those shoes and stay there for increasingly long periods of time, ultimately settling fully into the persona and lifestyle you have chosen and designed.

Based on what you know so far about who you want to be when your recovery is complete, spend some time each day (one to two minutes is plenty, more if you feel comfortable) imagining that your future stretches out ahead of you. On that road, path, or trail, imagine you can see the New You moving toward you. Hold the image and allow her to come as close as possible.

Sometimes you have to play make-believe in order to become the person you want to be.

Becoming the New You is a process that takes time not only to achieve, but also to get used to as an idea. Because you've lived as a survivor for so long, it would be reasonable to expect that your shift of self-perception might take some time to evolve from a place of powerless negativity to powerful positivity.

As you develop your ability to shift into "I can handle it!" mode and your new self, sometimes you will lack utter faith in the truth of those things or disbelieve that you already are or can be who you most desire. That's okay. In those moments, a great solution is to just out-and-out *pretend*.

When you act "as if," you role-play to explore what it would feel like and require for you to be exactly who you wish to be. Acting "as if " can be an extremely effective way to transition yourself into actually being the way you aspire to be, because it allows you to model the behavior you want. It's like trying on a pair of shoes and walking around the store: You don't yet own the shoes, but you're trying them out and imagining how they would feel if you did own them.

When you act "as if," you are behaving from a place of role-playing confidence. This engages your imagination, rehearsal mechanism, and immersion processes. In a place of expanded freedom, pretending allows you to develop tools, perceptions, successes, and experiences that show you who you can be. Then these skills naturally transfer into moments when you are yourself. From what you learn, you can build on these moments, enlarge your experience, and eventually become exactly that person you most desire.

Identify a quality or personality trait you would like to have. Study someone (you personally know or know of, or a character in a book or movie) who has it. See what clues you can pick up from that person's behavior and actions.

Then imitate that person: Pretend you too have that quality. What would you say? What would you do? What would you think? How would you behave, dress, play, work, etc.?

~~~

In acting "as if," you ask yourself to practice living the truth of something even though you admit you do not yet own it.

This behavior is very different from lying, which is deliberately telling yourself something you know to be false without admitting it.

When you act "as if," you develop necessary skills for handling problems, responding to fear-based thinking, and taking actions.

Think back over your life and the things you've learned to do. Riding a bike, for example. You didn't get on the bike and immediately ride like a pro. Instead, you acted as if you could do that: You pedaled and steered and kept practicing until you could ride like a pro.

> Sometimes releasing old PTSD habits begins by modeling the behavior you would like to become a pro at. What one habit do you feel ready to reduce? How can you act as if you've succeeded at that today?

~~~

Become your own superhero (in three [easy] steps):

- **Step One: Make a list of people you admire.** For each person, summarize the qualities and traits that person possesses that you respect and desire. Choose one person at a time and spend the day impersonating her or him: dress the same, listen to the same music, eat the same foods, talk, walk, and behave as she or he would. Approach every moment, interaction, conversation, errand, choice, and action as if you are that person. Inhabit and offer her or his opinions, perceptions, beliefs, and attitudes.

- **Step Two: After you have role-played the person you admire enough to feel comfortable taking on those qualities, adapt the feelings and thought processes you access from this perspective**

into your own self and life. Inhabit the feeling of being that other person while you *behave as you*. For a little while, you will act "as if" you have whatever qualities that person possesses (they may not feel natural). Eventually, however, you will become so familiar with those characteristics and how to access them in yourself that you will truly be acting as you.

- **Step Three: When you feel comfortable with this process, take it to an even deeper level.** Imagine that your Future Self already exists as fully and completely as the person you most admire. Prepare to spend the day impersonating your Future Self. Spend some time sketching out the specifics of what this would look like in all the details, as you did in Step One. Then approach every moment, interaction, conversation, errand, choice, and action as if you are this Future Self.

<center>~~~~~~~</center>

Your Ideal Self is rational and wise.

Buried deep within, you have an Ideal Self. This is true even if your trauma started at birth. This Ideal Self makes smart decisions and good choices, thinks of long-term objectives, and predicts short-term consequences. Dominated by the prefrontal cortex, this self sees the big picture of you and the relationships and world in which you engage.

Think of your Ideal Self as an older sibling; someone who is empathetic and loving, accepting and supportive, partnering and loving, protective—and super, super smart.

The more time you spend imagining this person, the more real she will become, the more access you will have to her, the more she can guide you.

At some point today, sit in a quiet space (close your eyes if that feels comfortable) and focus on the intention to invite your Ideal Self to enter the room. Perhaps she will appear right away, or perhaps it may take some time. When she shows up, invite her to come as close as feels comfortable. If it feels natural, engage her in conversation; ask any questions or for any guidance you desire. (If your Ideal Self doesn't appear, just practice being in a space of openness to her.) Repeat this exercise in whatever way it happens for you on a daily basis for the next thirty days.

~~~

Own your self-definition.

Your "I am" concept and statement are part of the belief system from which you are operating every moment.

Right now, write out the first statement that comes to mind: "I am..."

That's your healing-in-progress statement, and it's perfect. However you describe yourself today is 100 percent okay.

Now here's the good news—today, you have a choice. You can decide you will always be defined by:

- trauma and its effects
- many factors beyond trauma

Which will it be? The healed "I am" is an unmapped road that sits patiently beneath your feet. It can lead anywhere. "I am" is your compass. The more you practice and develop a comfort level with it and the possibilities it presents and represents and the stronger your post-trauma identity grows, the more control you have over how your life unfolds.

Imagine it's a few months from now, and you have achieved your recovery objectives. Take a moment to sit with the idea of who you will be. Then write out an "I am" statement *in that person's voice.*

~~~

Your beliefs are who you are.

What you believe influences your choices, guides your actions, and creates the world in which you live. Think your everyday experience is random and out of your control? Think again!

If you're miserable, hate yourself, and experience the world in a wholly negative way, then you can be sure that your beliefs about yourself and the world are incredibly negative.

Becoming fully aware of what you believe, plus the positive/negative ratio of your beliefs, helps to refine your recovery focus.

Give yourself a belief litmus test. Fold a piece of paper into three columns. Label them "Myself," "Others," and "The World." Write out as many beliefs about each as you can think of. Then ask yourself the following questions:

- How many beliefs are positive?

- How many beliefs are negative?

- How are these beliefs affecting the way you make choices and take actions?

- Assess each negative belief: How would it benefit you to shift this to a more neutral or positive perspective? For each negative belief, what would be a (slightly) more positive belief?

- Assess each positive belief you noted in the three columns: If you were going to embody them more actively each day, what would that look like? How can you make that happen?

~~~~~

You possess unique skills and qualities that naturally bring success in specific situations.

Over your lifetime there have been things that, as you did them, you knew you excelled at. Maybe that was growing turnips, mixing paint, skateboarding, or doing origami. Maybe it was sitting still and daydreaming, or tying your shoes with the perfect loop and knot.

These capabilities are sort of like your liver: Even when you don't think about it, you carry it with you everywhere, and (unless you abuse it) it's very willing to work when and how you need it to.

Suspend judgment about the value of what you've noticed you're good at. All that matters is getting back in touch with a part of yourself that is good, productive, and tied to a sense of your knowing, sensing, and feeling something positive about what it means to be you.

Your innate strengths exist regardless of how often you have recently used them. Imagine they've been frozen and are patiently waiting to be thawed. If the sun were to shine down brilliantly upon them, what would happen when the ice ran off in rivers of cold, fresh, flowing water?

Take a look at who you are today: What are you good at?

Make a list of five things you've been naturally good at over your lifetime. When was the last time you actively used these skills? Plan how you will use three of them over the next week.

〜〜〜〜

What you're good at defines you.

When you look at yourself as a PTSD survivor, the view can be pretty depressing—necessary to acknowledge, but not exactly uplifting—which is why the following idea is so very, very necessary.

Flip the self-definition equation by (a) defining yourself *solely* by what you're good at, and (b) acknowledging how that skill improves the life of, or is helpful to, someone else.

When you identify what you're good at and then share that natural tendency in a way that helps others, you deepen your self-definition as a person who can positively affect lives beyond your own. Feeling useful connects you to a sense of community, which develops a positive context for your place in the world. This can lead to purpose, mission, and a vision for the future.

Identify five things you're good at, plus three ways each one improves the lives of others. What would it take to share those gifts more than you currently are?

~~~~~

Sustaining your motivation and momentum for healing requires inspiration.

When challenges amplify what you *don't* want, it helps to have stimulation that keeps you tuned in to what you *do* want.

If right now you're thinking, "Beyond feeling better, I don't know what I want!" that impulse is A-okay. Most survivors initially can't see ahead. Being unable to imagine the future is very normal.

Whether you can or can't see ahead, you can deepen your perspective and feed your need to be inspired by looking outside yourself. The lives, accomplishments, and attributes of others can help you gain clarity about what's going on inside you. Since it's often easier to be clear about others than yourself, you can use an external perspective to clarify your internal one.

Identify someone (a friend, family member, colleague, acquaintance, media personality, fictional character) who lives, works, plays, thinks, acts, and/or behaves in ways you want to. Get clear on your desire. Name it: "I want to…"

Why do you want that? What does it mean to you? How would your life change if you had it?

Now is a great time to reintroduce yourself to the whole you.

With very little effort, you could list tons of adjectives describing yourself as a trauma survivor. Could you do the same for the rest of you?

Consider yourself in this moment. Make a list of things you appreciate about who you are *as you are today* (even if you feel a lot of disdain for that person). Dig deep and find some good in you. Enter your answers in your notebook, journal, or computer.

If you can't think of a single thing that you appreciate about who you are, try this approach: Take every action you do today and find a reason to appreciate what it means about you. For example, you opened this book. What positive quality does that mean you have? Name it. You spent most of the day in bed? What positive quality does that mean you have? Name it. You drank a glass of water? What positive quality does that mean you embody? Name it, and then continue...

Deepen this process: Ask others to share what positive qualities they notice in you. Then repeat the exercise by assessing yourself and your behavior and finding additional examples.

Connect to your Core Self.

Living disconnected from your authentic Core Self decreases your strength, courage, and confidence. Being disconnected also makes it more difficult to access resilience, productively utilize your imagination, and take necessary actions to move forward.

Trauma changed you the way snow changes a landscape: The snow can cover it completely, but the landscape itself (the ground, the hills and valleys, or flatness of it—its essential nature and composition) remains unaltered.

Despite what trauma has done to change you in terms of symptoms, lifestyle, and other shifts, the core of who you are still exists *unchanged*. If you were wired for compassion, you still are. If you were wired to be a musician, you still can be. If you were wired to be joyful, helpful, adventurous, or spiritual, those qualities still remain, waiting to be activated.

You have only to decide to cultivate a connection to who you were, or who you imagine you could have been, to start creating pathways of connecting to your Core Self again. In doing so, you increase your creativity, flexibility, and sense of personal grounding—all great bonuses that increase healing momentum.

> Who is your Core Self? Take a few moments to imagine what kinds of qualities define (or those you would like to define) your most authentic self. Make a list of everything that comes to mind. Place a star next to the five that are most important to you today. What can you do to connect to those qualities and exhibit them in your life this week?

Even when you finish your trauma recovery, you will still be in the process of constructing your post-trauma identity.

Your identity (r)evolution will continue as long as you live and breathe. While a lot of growth happens naturally without your designing it, some of the most important growth comes from the work you deliberately choose, founded on your desires and in alignment with evolving you in the direction you most want to go, regardless of obstacles along the way. Stretching yourself will be critical to future growth in ways that excite, challenge, and celebrate you.

Stretching means identifying new desires that continue to gently edge you out of your comfort zone and into territory that is unfamiliar. You don't grow by staying inside what's known; you grow by being bold enough to step outside what's familiar and bravely seeing what new situations require in terms of strength, confidence, and action. You want to always be capable of surprising yourself; stretching allows you to flex this skill in ways that further develop you as a person.

When you have settled into the idea of your post-trauma self, start looking around for the next step. Ask yourself the following questions, and let the answers guide you toward new decisions and experiences:

- What have I always wanted to do but have never made the time for?

- What have I always wanted to do but have been too afraid to try?

- What have I always wanted to have, be, or do, but others' opinions have stopped me?

- What part of myself do I really admire? How can I embody this part even more?

- Where in my life do I feel stifled? What would it take to feel like I'd been set free?

- What natural, healthy part of myself do I suppress? Why? How can I let that part become more active?

- How can I share my natural strengths in a way that benefits others?

- How can I use my natural strengths in a professional way?

- How can I use what I'm good at to continue to develop my post-trauma identity?

Celebrate who you are.

Healing often includes many painful moments. Facing fears and memories, disappointments and betrayals, plus the host of other uncomfortable actions you take to move forward, introduces many scary moments. The tendency in trauma recovery is to get lost in all of what brings you pain, grief, loss, and sadness; you forget that there are still good, honorable, respectable, and wonderful things about you.

Up to this moment, you've spent plenty of time criticizing and critiquing who you are. Probably, too, you've spent a lot of time memorializing, even romanticizing, the person you used to be or could have been. Today, turn in a new direction, one that might seem counterintuitive and yet has important and significant application at this moment in your healing journey.

> Identify five things that make you feel proud of yourself (come on, dig down and find them!). For each item, create one experience in which you honor it over the course of the next seven days.

You are here in this lifetime to be you.

A computer's operating system receives multiple updates related to revised programming and technological advances every year. As you grow emotionally, psychologically, and intellectually, your processing system (strategies, beliefs, meaning, perceptions, and interpretations) also requires updating.

When you change your perceptions, interpretations, applied meanings, and beliefs, you change your connection to the past. Doing so allows you to change who you are in the present, which changes the possibilities for your future. This can be done with the integrity of truth and honesty through a process of updating your point of view.

In this specific moment, your trauma(s) has passed. Even in the moment it occurred, it was, in itself, an objective occurrence. The event has zero power to create any kind of change in how you define who you are. The alterations you notice in your self-concept come directly from your own perfectly deserved, normal, and relevant internal physiological and psychological responses to trauma filtered through your neurobiology, belief systems, and meaning.

In every moment, you retain the capacity to reverse, revise, and overcome those changes.

You are here to express your self, your soul, your voice, your perspective, and your uniqueness through your entire life. You are meant to do this via choices and actions that make you feel good and true and necessary and real and purposeful, day after day.

> Identify one perception, interpretation, or belief that causes you discomfort and distress and that you know restricts your ability to move forward in feeling better. Examine the truth of what you identified. Knowing what you know now (as opposed to immediately after your trauma), what's a more updated way to look at it? What's more in alignment with who you want to be?

~~~~~

Let your soul sing.

Choreography to be danced to the music of "What I Want Is…" sung by Your Soul.

- **Step One: Identify five people you admire.** Consider the whole person: how she or he talks, thinks, acts, behaves, works, achieves, dresses, eats, etc. These can be actual people you know or people you know of; people who are alive and those who have passed. In your notebook, journal, or computer, outline what you admire about each person. What featured or dominant qualities do these people have that particularly resonate with you?

- **Step Two: When you complete the assessment of each person, turn to a new page in your notebook, journal, or computer.** Combine all of the traits, qualities, and characteristics you identified for each person: pull them together onto one page.

- **Step Three: Sit in a quiet place and slowly read over the list.**
  If these elements belonged to you, how would that feel? What
  would you look like, talk like, and act like? How would your life be
  different? How would that change who you are?

- **Step Four: From the list, identify the top ten qualities you'd
  like to own.** Decide to embody one trait at a time. If you were
  going to develop them in you, what would have to happen? What
  actions would you have to take? Develop a plan to incorporate one
  characteristic each week. Throughout the week, focus on that one
  new attribute and how often you can embody it.

PART FIVE

BUST THROUGH BLOCKS

Every PTSD recovery contains *splat!!!* moments. As awful as they feel, they all have a purpose. Also, they are *temporary*.

As you'll see in the following pages, blocks show up in recovery in a variety of ways. How you handle them has as many approaches as you have blocks. The most important thing to remember is this:

BLOCKS ARISE FROM FEAR.

The more hip you get to this concept, the more quickly you will develop a process for removing the block. It's all about recognizing the obstacle, identifying the fear, and creating resolutions that lead to outcomes that dissolve the block and open the way forward. Sound too general? Get ready to become very specific about how to overcome blocks arising from symptoms, outside sources, your inner critic, and different parts of yourself whose agendas collide.

WHAT STALLS PTSD RECOVERY?

Healing from PTSD can actually feel worse than living with it.

Making recovery especially hard are the "push me/pull me" internal conflicts that so often render you completely inert. Stuck between two opposing forces, you may feel you can't go forward or back. It's as if one part of you wants to heal, while another is willing to do just about anything but what recovery demands.

There are many reasons for internal conflicts to crop up. These are some of the more popular:

- **Healing upsets the status quo.** It takes a long time to learn how to manage and cope with symptoms. Once you do, it's nerve-wracking to engage in healing work that requires you to change the systems you've put in place to feel safe and in control.

- **Feeling emotions is painful.** To a certain extent, you've buried, numbed out, and cut off so many of your feelings that you live in an emotional dead zone. Healing requires you to come back to the land of the living, which is a necessary but excruciating process.

- **Letting go of your PTSD/trauma survivor identity is scary.** In the grip of trauma, you know who you are; letting go of that and trusting yourself to find another self-definition is frightening at a time when you need things to be comforting.

While conflicts can make things seem more chaotic, they actually serve a very real and genuine purpose: They force you to make a choice, form a commitment to, and take an action toward healing. Every conflict offers you an out; depending on your choice and how you resolve the conflict, you can either strengthen or weaken your recovery process.

Mull over your healing process so far. Where do you/when do you/what causes you to feel stuck between the part of you that wants to feel better and the part that wants things to stay the same? How have you responded to this in the past? Ideally, how would you like to respond? Look for an opportunity to do that this week.

~~~~~

Post-traumatic growth is defined by positive psychological change as the result of a challenging life experience.

Forget being perfect or having your progress and process happen flawlessly. Post-traumatic growth is about what you do with and how you respond to experiences in the past, present, and even your future. While the objective after trauma is to control as much as possible (about yourself, others, and the world), the lesson of healing is how to live a better, fuller, and more comfortable life by learning to exert control in more healthy ways: through the expression of your authentic Core Self's (not your fear-based self's) desires, choices, and actions. You achieve this when you relinquish control over the negative aspects of the world and its effects on you and claim control over the positive aspects of who you are and how you live.

It's all a lot like the way Thomas Edison developed the lightbulb: Legend claims it took over two thousand attempts to reach success.

In those moments when things go differently than you hoped, think of Edison: If he had allowed the unexpected to distract or dissuade him, you could be reading this page in the dark by the flame of a candle. Instead, Edison persevered.

You, like Edison, are an inventor, a discoverer in the realm of possibilities of your own recovery. Any self-respecting inventor knows that the only response to an unpredicted outcome...is a predicted determination to try again.

Along the way to healing, you will encounter obstacles. Develop your own personalized step-by-step process for how you'd like to handle them. In your notebook, journal, or computer, write out your process, and keep it somewhere you can easily access it.

Next steps come from clarity on missteps.

So much of healing is about tearing down (old beliefs and habits) and then building back up (new choices and actions). In the process of doing this, you build a new identity based on strength, courage, confidence, and clarity. Whew, it's a lot of work, but so worth it!

Every step you take—whether or not it brings the hoped-for results—has use and purpose. Imagine this: You are an explorer in unknown territory. You have no idea where the land dips, where sinkholes open, or where solid ground will hold your weight. Each step contains unknowns.

In your recovery, every step forward (including missteps) provides illumination into what feels good and what doesn't, what works and what doesn't, what you need and what you don't. This process also helps you develop essential elements that allow you to become more flexible, adaptive, and creative—all necessary components for being safe and in control in any future situation.

> Gaining clarity from missteps opens an opportunity for post-traumatic growth. The next time you feel you've made a mistake, ask yourself, "What do I know now that I didn't know before?" Follow that with: "How can I use this information in the future and to move ahead right now?"

Healing will happen only when you are ready for it.

But that doesn't mean you have to sit and wait. No matter how ready you feel, there are ways to interact with the recovery process and yourself that are supportive versus demanding, that can confirm your connection versus destroy it, and that pave the way to that ultimate day of courage, so that when it happens, you're ready to act.

- **Acknowledge, validate, and lessen the fear.** Recovery is S-C-A-R-Y. Facing the past, dealing with the memories and the flood of overwhelming emotion, containing a psychological experience so vast and enormous within the confines of a physical body so small and limited—all would challenge the courage of anyone. To move closer to feeling brave enough to heal, you will find it helps to shine a light on the fear that healing represents. Ask, "What's my biggest fear about talking (or healing, recovery, etc.)?" Listen to the answer and then methodically start identifying options to reduce the fear. You're more likely to engage in recovery when the idea of it produces a more neutral response.

- **More connecting, less nagging.** Jumping into recovery is a little like skipping rope: You have to get into the rhythm of it. Once you do, it's possible to jump in and keep time. Connecting with yourself outside pressure to heal allows for a stabilizing, supportive, non-trauma-related life rhythm. To access this, plan activities, outings, and plenty of time during which you focus on anything other than recovery. Find ways to relate to yourself (even if for only thirty seconds) as if PTSD does not exist. That is, as a whole person versus a survivor.

- **Educate and inform.** Being told by others what you "need," "should," "must," or "ought to" do doesn't necessarily relate to your specific history or present requirements. Only you know your deepest thoughts and feelings; they count in the recovery process and should be respected as guideposts in designating the chosen route. Educating yourself about trauma and recovery—and discovering what directly speaks to your experience—places the power back in you and can create a turning point in your healing process.

Are you ready to heal? Take some time today to mull over this question. Make a list of all the reasons why you are, plus a list of things that hold you back. Then identify what needs to change

to remove those obstacles. How can you create that process?
Who can help?

<hr>

**In every stage of recovery, there can be instant successes and
frustrating challenges—neither one decides your final outcome.**

Where you end up in the final phase of your healing largely depends on
how you respond to the unexpected:

1. *That was easy!* moment that
   lessens your focus

2. *What the $%*! happened?*
   moment that makes you
   question your ability to heal

3. *How long will this progress
   last?* moment that makes
   you doubt you can
   maintain the gains

You can keep yourself moving through each bend in the road by asking
one question: "How much do I want to reach my ultimate objective?"

If the answer is "Not much," then turn your energy toward reconnecting
to your healing purpose.

If the answer is "More than anything I've ever wanted in my life!" then
find ways to make one new choice and take one more action to either keep
you—or get you back—on track.

Support your motivation by reminding yourself why achieving
the desired results is important to you. Write out your answers
to these prompts and refer to them any time you need to keep
yourself focused:

- When I reach the end objective in recovery, I will
  be able to...

- At that point, I will be safer because...

- I will be more in control because...

- I will be more the person I most deeply wish to be due to the fact(s) that...

- By then, I hope that my life will change in these ways...

~~~~~

The PTSD recovery dance is tricky and complex.

One of the hardest things about PTSD recovery is that it feels as though you don't make constant forward progress. There are so many times when you work hard to move ahead just one lousy inch. Then, as you feel good about that, something happens—a trigger, a crisis; someone says something in a tone you don't like. The next thing you know, you're reacting instead of responding, and the slip/slide begins. Suddenly, *poof!* You're now two steps behind. Or are you? Consider this:

- **You can't go back.** In other areas of recovery, you've already discovered that it's impossible to go back to who you used to be. This is a fact; it doesn't change depending on the situation. Technically, you can't go back to who you were before your trauma, and you can't go back to who you were when you were "two steps behind," either.

- **You can only *feel* as though you've gone backward.** Your feelings, however, can whip around in and out of the same space all the time. So, you can feel the way you did when you were two steps back, but that's all it is—a *feeling* of being more depressed, out of control, anxious, panicky (or whatever applies to you) than you felt when you were feeling that you had moved ahead.

- **You can't unlearn what you know.** To move one step ahead means you've learned something new: a tool, a skill, a fact, an experience. Even if your emotions skitter, you still have that new knowledge, which means the knowledge/skill/fact/experience is yours; you own it, so you will always be at least one step ahead of the old "two steps back."

- **You're always receiving new information.** Even when you feel as though you're slipping back, you're receiving new information *that you didn't have two steps behind*. This information in this brand-new moment means the outcome can be wholly new too. This is a moment unlike any you've ever experienced, which means, technically, you've moved forward.

- **Familiar, old feelings happen in unfamiliar, new territories.** Relocation therapy doesn't work: Moving from one city or state to another doesn't mean you will never feel bad or unhappy again. It means you'll feel those things in a new geography that offers a new experience of those old feelings with new outlets and supports for it. The same is true in PTSD recovery. Feelings can *remind* you of another time you felt this way, but the truth is, you're in a new place this time.

- **You always have new opportunities to make new choices and take new actions.** The two-steps-back feeling is an opportunity for you to reclaim control. It's a moment that takes you by surprise and also offers you the option of feeling that feeling *and then* creating a different outcome this time around.

Think back to the last time you felt good about the progress you were making. What were you doing that made you feel that way? Jot down some notes so that, the next time you feel as though you're slipping back, you have action steps to catch you mid-step and bring you forward.

〜〜〜

Every obstacle has a reason for being.

Sustained PTSD creates many trauma-related conflicts, so it's no surprise that resolving those conflicts can be conflicting! Learning how to manage internal conflicts and find resolutions teaches you problem-solving skills that will serve you for the rest of your life.

Today, treat yourself kindly and use either of these approaches to lessen the internal conflict you may be feeling:

- **Honor both sides of the conflict.** Both sides of the conflict equation have relevant and valid concerns, desires, ideas, and opinions, and they offer important choices. Resist belittling yourself for having the conflict and instead embrace both perspectives. Ask yourself what each side is trying to do for you. What motivates their presence and interruption? Figure out how you can allow the underlying good intention (see page 40) of both to succeed.

- **Use your internal feedback mechanism.** When you experience yourself feeling better little by little, you know you're on the right track. If you're consistently feeling worse, interpret those experiences as messages letting you know that it is time to make a change in some part of your approach.

You have an internal feedback mechanism that will always answer every question. Suspend all fears and check in with your intuition. It will advise you what to do and how to move forward.

Explore these questions today:

- Are you on track?

- Are you responding to internal conflicts in appropriate ways?

- Are you moving in the right direction?

~~~~~

There are no accidents in what trips you up; every bump, block, or wall in recovery presents an important element that needs to be addressed.

When you come face to face with tough material in recovery, it's normal to resist. In fact, it's really smart. Resistance is a safety mechanism that pops up to let you know you're in territory that feels uncomfortable.

While trauma resolution is the objective, one of the biggest challenges in PTSD recovery is untangling the overactive fear response from the work that needs to be done. It's fair to feel the impulse to hold on, stay stuck, or run away. It's also fair for an outside perspective to challenge those actions. In addition, it's fair to respect the resistance impulse and work with it, rather than deny or try to eradicate it:

RESISTANCE = A BID FOR SAFETY

Any time it seems (or someone suggests) that you "want" to hold onto your trauma or stay stuck, it has zero to do with desire or choice; it has to do with fear...of change and your ability to handle the outcomes.

Acknowledge, validate, and appreciate any resistance you feel. A part of you is sending the message, "Whoa! We're headed into a place that feels very different. Are you sure you're ready for this?"

What ideas, topics, or issues are you resisting in your healing journey? In your notebook, journal, or computer, list as many as you can. How does each item on the list represent something that is important to you?

~~~~~

Beneath all resistance lies a deep well of fear.

What holds you back or stuck highlights important aspects of recovery that need to be explored. Those moments of resistance are road signs that (when appropriately worked through) lead you forward with greater confidence, skills, and knowledge.

A sample process for engaging with resistance includes these steps:

- **Identify the area of resistance.** You can resist an idea, action, belief, or thought. You can resist a person, memory, physical experience, emotion, or feeling. Take some time to notice what, exactly, you are resisting. Ask: "What am I trying to stay away from?"

- **Understand your resistance.** Examine the object of your resistance and discover why you want to get as far away as possible. Ask: "Why am I resisting this?"

- **Recognize the fear.** The prime driver motivating resistance is fear. Now that you know what you're resisting and why, notice the specific fear attached to that object. Ask: "What am I afraid of?"

- **Appreciate the fear and how it's trying to protect you.** Acknowledge that fear is trying to do something good for you. It may not always be appropriate, but the impulse is to keep you safe. Appreciate that impulse; thank the fear for its real message, which is *Be careful*. Ask: "In what way do I need to be careful?"

- **Strategize how to reduce and even eliminate the fear.** To move on, you will need to move fear out of your way. To do this, you will need a plan to keep yourself safe from what the resistance is warning you about. Ask: "What would make me feel more safe moving forward in this area?"

For each area of resistance identified here, ask yourself, "How does this perceived danger threaten who I am, who I will be, and what I am trying to achieve?" Then develop a strategy to protect those things.

~~~~~

As you change and become stronger and more effective, you will have thoughts, perspectives, ideas, responses, and opinions that continually lead you forward into new territory.

Some things will work, and some won't. Some recovery actions will yield the wished-for results, and some will yield unexpected results or challenges that weren't part of your vision. Some of those things that weren't part of your vision will fit into the overall outcome perfectly; some won't.

The plan in all of these actions and processes is to learn, explore, and discover who you are and will become. When you look back five years, ten years, and even twenty years from now, it won't matter if everything proceeded and evolved exactly as you thought it would. The only thing that will matter is that you got the job done, which means you freed yourself from the chains of the past and liberated yourself into a present and future in which it feels good to be you.

The process of change and uncertainty is ongoing in any life. Practice adapting to those situations: Look for low-stress opportunities to challenge yourself with the unexpected, so that your brain and self develop ways to synthesize new, unexpected information and make appropriate choices and actions.

~~~~~

Transcend fear so that you are large and the fear—like a small, annoying insect—can be dealt with any way you choose.

Today, test one of these processes for accepting, working with, and reducing fear:

- **Face the fear.** Our natural tendency is to run from frightening things. That's a biologically hardwired tendency and can go a long way to helping our survival as a species. In PTSD recovery, however, running away indulges avoidance tendencies (a PTSD hallmark) and so actually puts you deeper into PTSD rather than bringing you out of it. Healing means finding the courage to face the things that frighten you most.

- **Find a buddy.** All too often in PTSD, you assume (a) no one will understand, (b) no one feels the way you do, and (c) no one can help. News flash: You are part of a large crowd of people who feel exactly the same way you do. And there are many knowledgeable people who have ideas about how to help you feel better. Holding yourself in isolation allows the situation to feel like it's you versus the fear. You *and your posse* versus the fear is a much stronger position, whether that's allowing one person to support and help, or several.

- **Write it down.** Trauma creates chaos in your mind. PTSD is part of the process of how your mind struggles to create a new order. You can give this process a boost by organizing information. When the fears swirl through your mind, pin them down with words that are outside your mind. One great way to do this is to write out what your fears are. When you choose the language to express your feelings, you reclaim a very important element of control.

- **Say it out loud.** The things in your mind feel more intense, sound louder, and look bigger than they actually are. When you say these things out loud, you further the process of shrinking them down to size. Hearing the fear in the real world places it in a more proper context, which allows you to begin separating yourself from it. The more separated you become, the more the fear shrinks.

- **Make a plan.** Knowing what you will do and how you will handle frightening things shrinks fear. Having a strategy allows you to claim more control, which shifts you from powerless to powerful, which reduces fear. Think ahead into your fears and decide how you will respond to those situations should they occur.

Join the free Heal My PTSD forum for guidance, support, and connection with others who "get it" and are finding ways to face their fears: HealthUnlocked.com/HealMyPTSD.

~~~~

Fear creates chaos. Safety comes from things you can depend on.

When you redevelop your ideas about your recognition of and your experiences with safety, you counter chaos with calm. How can you do that at a time when you're always feeling on edge? The same way you create any success in PTSD recovery: by identifying small opportunities, choices, and actions that create oasis-like moments when your focus shifts from danger to safety in lasting, cumulative impressions.

Start being aware of positive, supportive, protective things you can already depend on. Examples to get you started include:

- a compassionate friend

- an animal's presence

- beauty in nature

- a moment of stillness

- a schedule

- the love of a family member

- the sound of a song that always makes you feel good

- the taste of something that makes you happy

- the smell of something that makes you feel comfort

Now that you're warmed up, take a moment to jot down things that make you feel safe that you can expect to happen in any day. Think about the people you know, the places you go, and the things you experience.

~~~~

One of the most common areas to get stuck in PTSD recovery is feeling suspended between the darkness and the light.

Since your trauma (and with PTSD symptoms), your conscious and subconscious minds focus on one thing: keeping you safe. The PTSD dark, in the way it keeps you isolated in a small, controlled world, can become a very safe-feeling space. But the dark is full of negative influences: memories and distorted beliefs, plus the myths and lies that trauma creates.

So, darkness is a place of familiarity (which feels good after trauma) even while darkness itself (in its oppression and your disconnection from the world) can feel bad. You want to get out of the darkness, but will you be safe if you do? And will you be able to function outside your current comfort zone?

The light, on the other hand, is like that shining carrot dangling just out of reach. When you seek PTSD recovery, you need something to look forward to and be drawn toward. Light represents all of your hopes, dreams, desires, wants, wishes, and every other good, exciting, and anticipated detail of the fantasy of your future life.

Imagining you can have and be and live in the light is healing (literally: this kind of thinking ahead engages your brain in positive aspects of imagination, which aid in neuroplasticity and cause brain change), while at the same time the possibilities—which open your life—can feel frightening. As your world increases in size, you have the opportunity to step forth and live in an incredible amount of freedom. This, of course, challenges your long-held safety precautions.

So, you want to step into the light, but do you have what it takes? And do you deserve it? The answers to these questions set the stage for forward movement.

What represents the light to you? Notice what feels good and what feels threatening about it. What would it take for you to move a little more toward the light? Identify what you need (to do) to move a fraction more in that direction; then take a comfortable action.

~~~~~~

Intense emotions are like highlighters in your brain: they let you know when you're in the vicinity of important details and concepts.

Your first impulse may be to turn away from or suppress intense emotions. Indeed, they can feel so overwhelming that anyone would want to get away as fast as possible. But here's why it's important to pay attention to them: You experience intense emotions when you're touching material that is important to you and your recovery process.

The intensity of your feeling increases in direct proportion to how relevant and significant the subject is to you. When you experience this feeling, the best thing to do is work your tools for emotional regulation (for example, breathwork, grounded posture) and then slowly approach assessing the emotion and its message.

The next time you feel an extreme emotion, grab a pen and paper or your computer and try this:

- Imagine the emotion is a person; name it.

- Categorize the emotion (such as "sadness"); write it down.

- Identify the thought that is causing the emotion; write it down.

- Look at the emotion and ask, "What important information are you trying to convey?"

By asking yourself that simple question, you gain further insight into the source of your discomfort. To begin alleviating it, ask these follow-up questions:

- "What do you want me to do?"

- "What action does that answer require?" Take one or more steps toward it.

Anxiety is a figment of your (overactive) post-trauma imagination.

To combat fear, you put in place repetitive habits, procedures, and processes designed to make you feel safe and secure. One such habit is worry about future situations—anxiety. Since anxiety looks ahead, it is always based on fiction rather than fact. It focuses on what you worry *might* happen, not on what will definitely occur.

Living in the habit of anxiety makes you feel safe because it fools you into thinking that:

AWARENESS = PROTECTION

While that's true in some situations, it's utterly false in others. The more you keep yourself on high alert, the less able you are to appropriately judge any situation; this leads you into greater danger.

To be truly safe, you need to be able to discern the difference between real danger and anxiety.

Combat anxiety by checking in with in-the-moment reality.

> When you notice you're feeling anxious, examine the facts and details of the situation. Make a list of the real threats— the objective, anyone-else-would-come-to-this-conclusion, inevitably damaging outcome(s). Then identify what would make you feel safer. Take three actions to reduce the threat(s) and give yourself a feeling of safety.

Depression and other post-trauma symptoms can create an attitude of dissonance about yourself and the life that might be available to you.

You've probably noticed there are weeks, months, or even years when you just can't seem to make yourself do the things you used to do, or know you should do to get your life back on track. There are many reasons for this response. Depression is one, plus:

1. The meaning of who you are has been altered by trauma, which means the things you used to like to do may not feel meaningful anymore.

2. The things you used to do might require a sense of freedom, an ability to focus, or an attitude of adventure/commitment/dedication that are not available to you right now.

3. Having a primary focus on threat and danger can make even the simplest activity seem overwhelming or unsafe and present a slew of unwanted uncertainties.

4. The world and what it has to offer can seem dramatically changed and unappealing when the emotion you know best is anxiety.

5. Your primary purpose now is safety and control; the less you do, the more you have of both (this feels like the truth, but is actually a myth).

Retraining your brain to live in harmony can happen through repetition.

Find something that makes you feel even the smallest bit good about being alive. Then create ways to experience that feeling frequently. This can mean adopting a pet, returning to an old hobby, picking up a new hobby, or granting yourself a much-longed-for wish.

To begin, think back to a moment or millisecond in which you have loved (okay, liked) being alive. What were you doing? How can you recreate that experience and sensation more often?

Pain illuminates what's important and challenges you to make those things a priority.

Although your impulse may be to shy away from pain, it can be very useful in your rediscovery process. What brings you grief, sadness, loss, and a sense of disconnection can actually educate you about your values, beliefs, and desires. Where there's emotional pain, there's love (of an idea, person, or thing), which means that, in every moment of such pain, you are simultaneously experiencing yourself as a being filled with love.

As odd as it may seem, pain helps you access an important part of yourself: your ability to love. From there, the process progresses by asking you to contemplate a question that holds the seeds of healing: What would bring the opposite of this pain?

Acknowledge all the ways in which you are in pain today. If you were going to feel the opposite of that pain, what would you feel? What would it take to create a small experience of that? How can you make that a priority over the next four weeks?

~~~~~

Expect, accept, and embrace grief and anger as rites of passage on your healing journey.

Trauma rips an enormous amount from any survivor. In the blink of an eye, security, safety, certainty, familiarity, confidence, and promises evaporate. Suddenly, you are left in the fog of destruction, missing what used to be true or what might have been and fearing what now is.

In this new landscape, grief and anger can profoundly proliferate because:

- You experience grief when something you love has been taken from you.

- You feel anger when you perceive a threat to your well-being.

- As you strive to reassemble your new world after trauma—and begin recognizing that the old world has been completely eradicated—you place even more value on what used to be and feel even more acutely the fear of what will or may be.

- For a long time, you may have been aware of the feeling of loss but avoided examining it. Or you may have been so numb that you didn't see, look at, or feel what had been disconnected due to trauma.

Your impulse may be to push grief and anger as far away or as deep down as possible. This is a mistake. Feeling worse comes from resisting the presence and truth of your responses; feeling better comes from acknowledging and integrating them.

In your notebook, journal, or computer, or on two pieces of paper, label one page "Grief" and one "Anger." Free write or make an individual list of all the things about which you feel grief and anger in your post-trauma world. For each item, identify one experience that would lessen the feeling just a little bit. Then ask, "In what way can I create that experience for myself?"

〜〜〜

Allow grief to rise and fall like waves on the ocean.

The intensity of grief comes and goes depending on what you're experiencing, what triggers have occurred, and how you feel about yourself in any given moment. Offer yourself the space to experience grief in any and all the ways it presents.

The five stages of grief described by Elizabeth Kubler-Ross are not a one-size-fits-all formula, but they're worth mentioning, as you may experience elements in any of the categories:

- **Denial:** Rejecting the idea that trauma or PTSD happened to you, or that any of yourself has been lost, changed, or altered since that event(s).

- **Anger:** Frustration that this experience has happened to you.

- **Bargaining:** Offering to a higher power that you will do X in return for this not having happened, or for your not having to do some really tough work to see changes and find relief.

- **Depression:** Being too sad to do anything toward healing this loss.

- **Acceptance:** Acknowledging "what is" and developing a plan to move forward.

According to this list, which phase do you feel you are in? What needs to happen for you to move through this space? What steps can you take toward that?

~~~~~

The more significant the loss, the more intense the grief.

Emotions are live entities that manifest through your interpretation of an experience. While your emotions are separate from who you are, they are a living and breathing sub-element that deserves to be noticed and respected.

When you first begin allowing yourself to thaw the numbness and experience feelings, you may notice that what you feel is more intense than you expected. That makes sense: For a long time you may have been feeling less than was real because you deadened yourself emotionally. While it takes effort, you can become a master at managing your emotions.

One way to expand yourself in this area is to understand that the strength of your emotions reveals what issues are most important to you. The more you let yourself feel what matters to you and the more connected you become to the priorities and internal drivers that motivate your choices and actions, the more you discover what you need to overcome trauma and create a life and self that feel good.

Connecting your past, present, and future emotional cues forms the basis of your post-trauma identity.

> Identify a thought that brings up a great deal of grief, anger, or shame. For the next twenty minutes, enter in your notebook, journal, or computer whatever comes to mind in relation to this prompt:
>
> "I am so upset about this because it means..."
>
> Based on the information you discover from this exercise, decide how you will transform the meaning into something that is more useful, productive, and supportive of your recovery. That is, if the meaning is "...it means I am unlovable," what can you do to start exploring the opposite—what indicates you are lovable—which will then open possibilities to change the meaning?

~~~~~

Anger represents one universal element: the perceived threat of danger.

The expression of anger has three components:

- **Physical:** Your body responds in typical fight-or-flight fashion with increased adrenaline, heart rate, blood pressure, and tightening muscles.

- **Cognitive:** Your mind creates an understanding of how you perceive and think about the thing that is angering you. (Hint: This is where your control lies.)

- **Behavior:** Your actions express your rage.

At the base of anger is fear; at the base of fear is powerlessness; at the base of powerlessness are the demons of the past and the idea "I can't handle it!"

A hard-wired survival skill, anger can be triggered by any situation that makes you feel jeopardized, including any moment that makes you feel fear, shame, guilt, embarrassment, or sadness. You can see anger as part of the fight-or-flight response.

Many survivors actually use the energy of anger to help propel them into feelings of empowered action in recovery. Transforming anger and fear into less aggressive, more enabled action is one of the ultimate areas where you learn to shift yourself from powerless to powerful.

Feeling threat or danger requires a response that moves you toward safety. Developing a habit of courage allows you to tap into a part of yourself that can keep you safe without living in a state of anger.

> To endure your trauma, you had to access the bravest part of you. How did you do it? How can you utilize elements of that process today?

What you grieve or rage against (and for how long and in what way) clues you in to what values you prize and how you like them to manifest in your life.

How often do you let yourself acknowledge pain, allow it to come close to you and then settle within you?

Immediately after trauma, there may not have been room (nor may it have been appropriate) for you to enter the intensity of grief or anger. You've done a great job of harboring it. Now it's time to process. As intense emotions, grief and anger provide much insight into who you are and what matters to you in terms of what you love and what you fear.

Seen from this perspective, grief and anger become very useful tools in rebuilding your life after trauma: They help identify what fuels your post-trauma responses, which means they also help identify what needs to be resolved to create change.

> The next time you feel grief or anger, explore them for insights into what you want, need, or require:
>
> - **Grief:** Ask, "What have I lost? Why was that important to me? What would have to happen for me to reclaim the feeling of it again?"
>
> - **Anger:** Ask, "What do I feel threatened by? What do I need to protect myself from?" Then take a less aggressive, healthier, and more effective action to lessen the fear.

~~~~~

Shame drives the fear of not being good enough, as well as a sense of humiliation.

Shame can make you hide, be silent, and deepen your sense of alienation. To begin combating shame, you need to understand that shame:

- is an emotion that is tied to *the person you feel you are*, rather than a specific behavior

- comes from an imagined defect in who you are (that's right, *imagined*)

- finds strength in the personal (the meaning you ascribe to a situation), as well as the attitude of the culture in which you live

- is driven externally, often by a fear that others will discover what you are most trying to hide (versus guilt, which is driven internally by a disruption in your own moral code)

Because trauma creates so many lies, myths, and distortions, you can easily lose sight of fact and reality. That's when shame can really sink its teeth in and start shaking you around.

Explore your personal shame resolution strategy by testing these options:

- **Add some gray.** Shame can feel enormous and incredibly catastrophic, but that's just it: Shame is only a feeling tied to a thought. The next time you feel shame, pause for a moment, take a step back, and identify the thought that preceded it; write it down. Trauma causes black-and-white thinking, which can lead you to accept that shame statement. But there is no black or white in the real world; there are always shades of gray. Look at the statement you wrote out. Shade in some gray: Write three other, opposite interpretations of the situation/moment/idea and try on the new thoughts they produce.

- **Explore.** Name, clarify, and organize your thoughts by exploring your shame. Take some time to think about these questions:

  a. What is the shame about, specifically? (List as many statements as you can.)

  b. What's the first time you remember feeling this shame?

  c. Who made you feel this way?

  d. What perceived personal defect do you feel the shame comes from?

  e. Objectively speaking, how accurate/true is that perception?

  f. What's an opposite perception?

g. List some reasons why your answer to that last question might be true.

- **Define and describe.** What do you feel the shameful issue means about you? Get a pen and paper or your notebook, journal, or computer, and write for as long as you can to get a full description: State what you are ashamed of; then write what it means about you. The more clarity you have around this subject, the more efficiently you'll be able to work with it. When the description is written, assess it: How accurate is what it says about you as a person overall? How do you know this is true? What would an objective observer say? What would an opposite meaning be? How accurate could it be?

- **Take a step back.** Imagine you can meet the part of you that is struggling with shame around this subject. Invite that part to enter the room. Spend some time observing this part. What do you see? What's the truth about the shame, where it came from, and what it means about this part of you? Write a letter offering empathy, understanding, and compassion to that part.

~~~

Recognize your response to feeling overwhelmed.

As with most feelings, before you experience a full-blown emotional response, you will have clues that a volcanic buildup is occurring. In lessening your feeling of being overwhelmed, it helps to become clear on the signs sent by your body and mind to alert you that overload is approaching.

Think back to the last time you felt the *whoosh!* of an overwhelming sensation. Answer the following questions:

- What were you doing when this happened?

- What were you doing immediately prior to this happening?

- What were you thinking?

- How did your body feel?

- What were your thoughts and feelings the moment the feeling of being overwhelmed began?

- What type of situation were you in?

- What was frightening you?

- What were you trying to accomplish?

- How many tasks were you juggling at once?

- Who were you with?

As much as you can, chart the twenty-four hours prior to that overwhelming feeling. Notice any recurring or intrusive thoughts, any uncomfortable body sensations, and any erratic or different behaviors and moods. Deliberately look for and notice what changes occurred between the moment(s) before you felt the overwhelming sensation and the full-on blow. These are clues that can help you notice, respond, and deflect more quickly in the future.

> Practice as many elements of this exercise as possible for the next four weeks. The more aware you become of your signals that let you know you're beginning to feel overwhelmed, the more you will recognize them and be able to interrupt the feeling by taking action in the moment(s) prior to losing control.

Beliefs create your world.

What you believe can stall, crash, and halt your healing, or lift you up and carry you over your worst day.

Pause for a moment right now and make sure your beliefs are helping, not hindering, your healing. Ask yourself:

- What do I believe is true about me?

- What do I believe is true about my life going forward?

- What do I believe is possible for me?

- What do I believe is possible in my recovery?

- What do I believe about other people in my life?

- What do I believe about other people in the world?

- What do I believe about the world at large? Complete this statement: "I believe..."

When you identify a belief that stunts your progress, recognize it as resistance. Turn to page 193 and put it through the resistance process to begin transforming it. Then turn to page 144 to learn how to replace a limiting belief with one that more appropriately supports your healing efforts.

~~~~~

What are you doing—or not doing—because of what you believe?

Believing ideas based on *You can't*, *don't*, or *won't* means you automatically accept limits in PTSD recovery. When these ideas are core beliefs—dominant ideas that dictate your available choices and actions—then healing feels like dragging a pack of elephants behind you.

PTSD recovery gains momentum when you identify core beliefs, verify their accuracy, and strategize how and in what way they affect your daily behavior. Here's a quick reference guide for recognizing core beliefs:

- Identify a behavior or feeling.

- Notice the thought that drives the behavior or precedes the feeling. (Ask, "What thought made me feel or act this way?") Write it in your notebook, journal, or computer.

- On a scale of 1 to 10 (10 being strongest), ask yourself how strongly you believe that thought. (If it ranks between 8 and 10, it's a core belief.)

Using these answers, you can identify major drivers in your PTSD behavior. Changing negative core beliefs will change your choices and consequently your actions.

Use the preceding three steps to identify one of your negative core beliefs and write it down. Now imagine that, tomorrow morning, you wake up and that belief has been transformed into a new belief that wholly supports your recovery process. (For example: "I can't let go of my trauma" transforms to "I am (open to) letting go of my trauma.") In your notebook, journal, or computer, restate the belief in its new form. What proof exists that this new belief might be true? What three actions can you take that support the new belief?

HOW TO OVERCOME THE MOST COMMON OBSTACLES

PTSD recovery is all about trial and error.

There are zero guarantees, zero prescriptions, and zero sure bets. In lieu of all that, you must proceed like an adventurous explorer in uncharted territory: Strap on your backpack, slip your compass in your pocket, and strike out in the direction that feels most promising, knowing you will keep going until you reach the desired landscape.

No matter what you're trying to achieve in this part of your healing journey, the method is the same:

- Identify objectives.
- Make a choice.
- Outline a strategy.
- Implement action.
- Assess results.
- Tweak strategy.
- Make a new choice.
- Take a new action.
- Repeat.

You are a unique individual. Your process for everything will be specific to you. Others can make suggestions, but you know yourself better than anyone. Trust the knowledge you receive when you check in with your deepest and most knowledgeable self—and then work with it.

> Sit in a quiet space. If it feels comfortable, close your eyes. Breathe in deeply five times. Then invite your most knowledgeable self to enter the room. Invite that self to come closer and closer, to stand or sit beside you. Be in each other's presence for as long as feels comfortable. Receive any information or message offered.

~~~~

Decide to go deeper into recovery work.

It's human nature to look at a difficult task and procrastinate until you have no choice but to go ahead and do it. In trauma recovery, procrastinating can be dangerous. Waiting until you have no choice usually means getting yourself into a place of even blacker despair. This makes healing choices and actions seem increasingly difficult, the hurdles higher, and recovery further off.

The more you allow PTSD symptoms to exist, the more difficult (yet still possible) they become to reduce and eliminate. It's better to take care of a problem when it's big enough to see and small enough to fix.

> Identify a recovery task, topic, or action you have been putting off. What's one small step toward doing it that you can take today?

~~~~~

The past does not predict your future.

An assumption is the belief that *if* something happened one way in the past, *then* it will happen exactly that way again, every time, in the future. The problem with believing in the consistency of if/then statements—and using them to inform your choices and actions—is that often they can be *wrong*. In fact, assumptions can lead you to decision-making processes that are entirely insubstantial. You may think, "The last time I tried to stop biting my nails, I started pulling out my hair instead. Better to bite my nails!" So you decide not to attempt reducing your nail-biting because you're afraid of the side effects.

However, if you have done some diligent healing work since that last attempt, then you may be at a point where you can actually stop biting your nails with courage, strength, and zero negative side effects.

Assumptions are fairly easy to spot, since they are unsubstantiated expectations. Dispelling them can also be fairly easy when you ask yourself the following questions:

- What experience in the past makes me believe this will happen in the present?

- Where is the *objective proof* that what happened in the past will happen now?

- How possible is it that there might be an alternative outcome?

- What do those possible alternative outcomes look like?

- What makes me know other outcomes are possible?

- What can I do to make the alternative outcome more likely?

Become aware of how often you employ if/then thinking. When you notice it, take some time to apply the preceding questions to shift to a more productive thought process.

A well-placed misinterpretation can inadvertently stall your recovery process.

In the Small World ride and exhibit at Disney World, the song says, "A smile means friendship to everyone." The reason is that, around the world, we all *interpret* the curve of upturned lips as a gesture of friendliness.

Objectively speaking, however, upturned lips are just that—a set of muscles curled in an upward position. It is your interpretation of that gesture that gives it the friendly meaning. An interpretation is an opinion or judgment that you form about an event.

In healing, it's important to be aware of how interpretations interfere with your process. Here's a simple example:

You may feel that the act of looking back, holding onto, and thinking about the trauma is a way to honor and respect yourself and others who lived through the event. It was an important experience; you can't just pretend it doesn't matter. So, if someone were to suggest that you "let it go," you may become incensed by the suggestion of such betrayal. You interpret the suggestion as offensive, which makes you feel the need to appreciate and honor the past even more. Consequently, you may find yourself holding on more tightly than ever, as your unhappiness or post-trauma symptoms increase and bring your healing to a halt.

Now, in the same example, let's look at the other side of how interpretations work. What if you were to interpret the suggestion to "let it go" as permission to honor yourself, others, the past, and your survival by releasing the pain you've been carrying for so long? Suddenly, this new interpretation opens up possibilities and forward motion.

In transforming interpretations, you must first identify what is important to you. In the preceding example, it's important to honor and respect the past. Second, identify how you can maintain that importance while finding a new perspective and action (i.e., creating a release ritual retains the importance while offering a different outcome).

Use these questions for reframing two interpretations today:

- What's another way to look at this?

- What's a different story to explain this?

- What would someone else say about this?

- What's the opposite view?

- How can I look at or understand this in a more healthy, compassionate, or supportive way?

~~~~~

Recovery is about allowing yourself to be you—and embracing who that is in any moment.

Self-criticism is a natural part of PTSD. So natural, it should be part of the diagnostic criteria! Renegotiating that critical perspective becomes a major part of the PTSD recovery process.

Naturally, your response to trauma makes you question everything—including yourself. Naturally, you may not like the answers you receive when you do any type of self-assessment.

Instead of hating or forever doubting yourself for the shortcomings you find, embrace them as things you now know that you can move toward changing and correcting and from which you can grow into a stronger person.

Spend some time listening to your self-talk. How often are you mean or unkind to yourself? Would you talk to a friend the way you talk to yourself? How often do you focus on the negative so that the positive ceases to exist?

Start making some adjustments to your inner voice that tone down, soften, or eliminate your most harsh self-criticisms. Replace ideas with understanding kindness ("Of course, I think this because...") or notice the benefit that unkind self-talk brings you (e.g., motivation). Then find another way to achieve the same outcome without the self-flagellation.

Be nice(r) to yourself.

You're dealing with and juggling a lot. The temptation is to lose patience, berate yourself with truly mean thoughts, and become frustrated when yet another symptom ruins the day.

You can create a much more powerful healing space by interrupting that kind of programming:

- How often do you **reward** yourself just for waking up in the morning and being willing to face another day?

- How often do you **appreciate** the fact that, despite what happened in the past, you still hope for a better future?

- How often do you **thank** yourself for showing up and seeking ways to feel better?

Doing any one of these things can make you feel just a little bit better/ good, which translates to a chemical change in your body that increases neuroplasticity, enhances your mood, and amps up energy that moves you further ahead in recovery.

Step One: Today, decide to be kinder to yourself. What would have to happen for you to make good on that intention? How can you implement that as a daily practice over the course of the next four weeks?

Step Two: Offer yourself a reward, write yourself a thank-you note, or show your appreciation through a deliberate gesture.

The more you believe in the negative perspective of your inner critic's voice, the more you will feel powerless, ineffective, and worthless.

Every mind houses a negative voice driven by fear, the desire to be in control, and the message, "You're not good enough!" In addition, the inner critic of a survivor is full of the myths, lies, and distorted thinking installed by trauma.

Because the messages you receive from this voice are unkind and hurtful, your negativity bias may tempt you to listen to them more than anything else. This is why developing a separation between you and your inner critic is an important step in reclaiming your personal power.

Remember this: Your inner critic is not you; she is a part of you. Being clear on the boundaries and differences inherent in that dynamic allows you to begin disentangling yourself from being ruled by her.

Try any of these actions to create a sense of separation:

- **Choose a name.** Naming your inner critic lets you both see very clearly that you are two separate entities.

- **Choose an image.** It may not yet feel like it, but you are bigger, stronger, and more effective than your inner critic. Find an image that conveys who she is. Print it or cut it out and place it somewhere visible so that it reminds you on a daily basis how paper-thin and small she really is.

- **Offer thanks.** Behind the critic's unkindness is a good intention. Acknowledge that she is actually trying to do something helpful by specifically naming what that help is. For example, say, "Thank you, Leah, for motivating me to get to out of bed today." Then take a complementary action.

- **Dismiss.** If you feel ready to put your foot down and convey a prolonged silence, say, "Pack your bags and go on a nice vacation." In your mind, watch your inner critic leave the room, close the door, and take off for some far-off destination. Or a simple "Not now" can buy you temporary silence in the moment when you most need it. Couple this directive with imagining that your inner critic (reluctantly) slinks away to hang out under the bed, under the desk, in the closet, or in another room.

Beginning to work with your inner critic means acknowledging her presence without judgment. The next time you hear that critical voice, resist the impulse to believe it, and, instead, just nod and say, "I hear you."

~~~~~~~

The real motivation of your inner critic is to help you.

The more you attempt to push something away, the more strongly it has to push back to get your attention. Resisting your inner critic is like saying, "Come on, I dare you!" And she, playing on your fears and anxieties, ups the game and brings on more drama than you could have imagined.

Welcoming her removes a level of resistance, which frees up your energy for more productive use.

Conversely, a major law of living is that you bring to yourself more of what you think about. This means that, the more you think about how much you hate your inner critic, and the more you furiously think, "Knock it off, sister!" without getting results, the more you bring to yourself feelings of angst and unrest.

The more you fight your inner critic, the more you fight—period. Saying instead "I understand you love me and want to make sure I'm safe" draws that voice under your wing; from there, you can begin working together instead of against one another.

The truth is that your inner critic really is about love for yourself. She wants the best for you; she just doesn't communicate in a way that allows you to hear the positive message behind what she says. You hear, "You're not worth it!" and shrink back. And why wouldn't you? It hardly sounds as though you're being asked to stand up, take back control, and prove you are worthwhile. But that's exactly what your inner critic is trying to convey.

It would be so much easier if she would say what she really means, which is, "I love you, and I'm afraid that if you don't take a stand in this situation, you will really get hurt. So, please, take some positive and healthy action." The poking and prodding of your inner critic can either goad you into movement or sink you in the quicksand of inaction, depending on how you understand the subtext of the messages being sent.

There is a very real benefit to the negative point of view: The constant needling actually challenges you to do better, be better, and strive for more. Turning your inner critic into your coach transforms this from a negative dialogue to a positive collaboration, which can be enormously powerful in infusing your recovery with an added boost of anabolic (positive, rejuvenating) energy. To get the most out of this benefit, you will have to coach your critic to become your coach. This means opening a dialogue in which you are in charge.

Try this:

- **Receive the real message.** The next time you hear the voice of your inner critic, resist the impulse to believe what she says (i.e., "You're worthless!"). Say to yourself, "I'm receiving a message that will keep me safe."

- **Interpret the meaning.** Fill in the blank from your inner critic's perspective: "I love you, and I'm afraid that if you don't choose to [*fill in an appropriate choice*] in this situation, you will really get hurt. So, please, [*insert your name*], take some positive and healthy action."

- **Identify the action.** Imagine it in great detail. Then, notice all of the options you have for taking it.

- **Reclaim control.** Reduce and eliminate the need for the unkind voice by hearing and acting on the message below the words. Choose an option and take steps toward implementing it.

- **Invite suggestions.** Critics always look at the past; coaches look from the present toward the future. What you want is a coach who can help strengthen you in future moments. If you're feeling remorse over something in the past, ask your inner coach, "What do you want me to do next time?" When your coach lapses into the critic and offers all the things you did wrong in the past, gently stop the conversation, remind your coach that you're talking about the future, and encourage ideas that offer support for later actions.

- **Embrace constructive criticism.** When you assign your coach a task, she can turn into your support rather than your obstacle. One way to put your coach to good use is to invite feedback on any plan. Let loose your inner coach's critical perspective to shake up a plan; find its weaknesses; and point out where, how, and why things need to be changed so the outcome will be stronger and more positive.

The next time you hear the voice of your inner critic, set the actual words aside and look for the subtextual meaning: What is she afraid of? What does she want you to do?

～～～

Recovery happens in action.

Freeze mode is a common experience for PTSD survivors. On one level, it comes from your brain's response to trauma: You can activate to fight or flee... or your brain can shut down, overwhelmed by experience, and, turtlelike, withdraw into its protective shell.

When you are caught in the prolonged PTSD trauma loop, the freeze response can easily become a part of how you feel daily. One way to bust out is to remind yourself to make simple choices and take small actions. Even the tiniest act interrupts the freeze response and nudges your mind and body into an experience of motion that can turn into momentum.

> Observe the various arenas of your life: family, friends, work, religion, etc. In what areas do you most wish to see a change in your experience and behavior? What one (small) action could you take to test the waters of change?

～～～

You can change your mind, brain, and body responses.

While it may not always seem like it, you do, in fact, possess what it takes to control your mind and emotions. True, learning to implement and appropriately wield that control—with a degree of intention and ease—can take time. True, you will have to undo, overcome, and interrupt deeply ingrained mind and body patterns that have thus far interfered with your control. Still, the essence of your ownership remains constant. In fact, that ownership is one of the most important discoveries you will make in recovery.

Remembering and/or learning how to do that requires you to develop skills that teach you how to reclaim control. One way to do this is to change the pictures you see, the thoughts you think, and the actions you take.

Imagine a situation in which you wish you had more control.
Pretend you can see the scene on a movie screen in your mind.
You are the director: Play the movie forward, putting in all of the
necessary changes so that the scene unfolds exactly as you wish.
Practice this three times a day for thirty consecutive days.

Note: *Develop this process related to instances of low urgency
first, so that you can utilize it effectively in regard to more
stressful situations once you've developed a level of proficiency
with the process.*

~~~~~

Challenge yourself.

In the avoidance perspective of post-trauma life, you're motivated to
move away from things deemed dangerous or threatening. But here's the
problem: If your whole life is about avoiding threat, then you never really
live. In fact, if your caveman ancestor had seen the tiger, been scared of it,
and then decided never to come out of his cave again, you wouldn't be here;
he would have died of hunger—and the power of his fear.

Instead, your ancestors found strong and empowered ways to come out
of the cave. Some of those ways even included learning to kill the tiger, which
means you can do the same.

Identify a habitual situation that brings you negative results.
Now challenge yourself to attempt, address, approach, or
handle it in a fresh/creative/new/opposite way. What will it take
to do that? Who can help?

~~~~~

See, feel, and be *big*.

Smallness is a viewpoint fueled by powerlessness.

During your trauma, you felt helpless. That feeling, in fact, became embedded deep in your body and mind. Today, that sensation of powerlessness continues to activate and create in you similar feelings of being small and ineffective. The longer you allow that to continue, the more you will feel stuck and unable to overcome the past.

PTSD recovery requires you to do things differently than you have been. Try this:

- Close your eyes and imagine yourself in a movie theater with an enormous IMAX screen. Allow a neutral picture to form on the screen, e.g., a tree.

- Now walk yourself as close to the screen as you can get. Feel how small you are next to the big picture.

- Then feel yourself easily, automatically, naturally, and gently begin to grow...up. With effortless lightness, your legs extend, longer and longer so that you grow taller and taller, and even taller still.

- Allow yourself to continuing growing up until you are as tall as the screen itself. Notice how everything looks now that it's at eye level. Look down and see how far below the rest of the theater is. Take time to notice how far away the floor is, how small the seats look, etc.

What do you notice from this height? How does it feel to be this big? Step into the screen and let the scene unfold...

Slow down!

Going full throttle in recovery causes a pile-up wreck worthy of the Indianapolis 500 about 99.99 percent of the time. Pushing too hard without allowing your brain to rest, forcing yourself into uncomfortable territory without finding ways to manage your responses, and driving yourself to achieve results add enormous pressure that amplifies anxiety and leads to less desirable outcomes and the mother of all obstacles: the Meltdown. Avoid being thrown off-track in this way by discovering what it feels like to slow down.

Caution: Slowing down will feel uncomfortable! In fact, it can feel downright scary. Moving fast means you feel more in control much of the time, because it allows you to feel numb. Slowing down means you'll feel more of your emotions, which, for a period of time, may make you feel more out of control. However, this will be a key moment: The more you feel, the more you heal.

Whether it's slowing down your mind, body, expectations, emotions, or desires, developing the slow-down skill is a major step in reclaiming control.

> Begin building a slow-down habit in just ten seconds a day: Sit still for ten seconds and notice how you are able to do that. Set a timer, watch the clock; however you want to accomplish this is fine. Do it six times a day for four weeks. When you feel comfortable, increase to twenty seconds, then thirty, then a minute, two minutes, five minutes, etc.

~~~~

Confidently acknowledge and transform emotions.

Everything about your body is designed to let go: Your skin and hair shed and regenerate, your tiniest cells respire, and your digestive system eliminates. The same is true for your emotions; they are energy that is meant to be released. The more you hold onto or suppress them, the more they can stall your progress.

Instead, become skillful at releasing and transforming emotions by interacting with them.

The next time you feel an intense emotion, try this:

1. Breathe into it and say, "I have a valid reason for feeling this way because…"

2. Imagine this feeling is circling your body, looking for a way out. Identify what would be the quickest way to release it (e.g., exhaled on your breath, seeping like sweat from your skin, zooming out through your ear canal).

3. Let that process happen; observe the entire action for as long as it takes. Trust that it will end.

4. Redirect your focus to a pleasant/peaceful image.

~~~~~~

Bust out of limiting beliefs.

Limiting beliefs are "truths" you tell yourself about yourself, your life, and the world that place limits on what you can and cannot do. They come in many shapes and sizes and will, if you allow them to remain, always stop you from achieving your desires because they offer ideas (excuses!) for why things can't happen the way you want them to.

For example: *I'm broken and can't be fixed.* In six puny words, the world just shrinks down to a speck in the universe.

But what if it doesn't? What if the belief is false?? In that case, the possibilities are *limitless.*

The tricky thing about limiting beliefs is that they can be developed, supported, and even expanded by your inner critic, assumptions, and interpretations, not to mention the outside world. Recognizing, reevaluating, and releasing limiting beliefs offers a powerful recovery process because it opens up room for opportunity.

Removing limiting beliefs from your healing will require you to identify their existence and then transform them through a process guided by the following questions:

- What is the limiting belief?

- How is it hurting you or holding you back?

- Where did this limiting idea come from? How reliable is that source?

- Who else holds this belief?

- How much do you want this "truth" to be false?

- What proof exists that the limiting belief is false?

- What would be a more positive, alternate belief?

- What (small) proof do you have that lets you know this alternate belief might already be true?

- What will this new belief allow you to achieve?

- Why are those results important?

- How will those results change who you are?

- How will they change the way you live?

- What action can you take to embrace and embody the new belief?

- When will you take that action?

- Who can help you take that action?

- What further proof would deepen this belief?

- How can you get that proof?

Make a list of "I can't..." statements related to PTSD recovery. Then prioritize them in order of how much they affect important aspects of how you move forward.

Take the first one and put it through the preceding list of questions. Rephrase the "I can't" to an "I can" statement.

Brainstorm (or ask friends and family for suggestions): What would have to happen in order for that new statement to be true? With the list of action steps, implement the first one and start belief-busting.

~~~~~

Make some ground rules.

You're used to being, living, and accepting yourself as a survivor. That means you live by survivor rules. For example, see if any of the following statements describe some of the rules you consciously or unconsciously live by:

- *It's better to isolate myself than to be around others.*

- *I have to hide my symptoms as much as possible.*

- *I have to accept that I am damaged.*

- *I must endure life from a less-than feeling.*

- *I must learn to live with PTSD symptoms instead of expecting them to go away.*

In your notebook, journal, or computer, add your own rules.

Trauma and "the rules" hold you back, but they don't wholly define you, and they're definitely not the sum total of who you want to be or can and will become.

Imagine you can chuck the old rules. What would be the new ground rules for how you live, feel, think, behave, experience, love, work, and create in the world?

Write some new rules:

- Draft a list of ground rules for how you would like to live.

- Then give them a respectable home in the real world. (Print out the rules and tape them onto your bathroom

mirror or refrigerator door. Laminate them and place
them in your pocketbook or briefcase. Record them in a
notebook, journal, or computer you carry with you.)

- Share them with someone you trust and add any
  suggested ideas that seem helpful.

The list will be helpful only if you interact with it. Allow it to
guide you by turning it into something that you can connect with
to inform your choices and actions throughout the day.

~~~~~

Examine the good.

The PTSD mindset is incredibly one-sided, but that's not the state
of the natural world, and the natural world is the one in which you live.
Rain balances sunshine; heat balances cold; sky balances earth; darkness
balances light.

For everything you feel hate, shame, embarrassment, and guilt for there
is an equal and opposite aspect of who you are that you can feel proud of,
encouraged by, appreciative of, and thankful for.

When was the last time you bucked the PTSD habit of looking at the bad
and truly noticed—heck, even *examined*—the good? Negativity and self-
criticism are the default setting in PTSD-land, but you can be more creative
than that.

If you were going to appreciate who you are today or who you
have been along the way, what qualities would you be glad
you possess?

~~~~~

Filter the voices around you.

The force of messages coming from external sources carries a big impact. When you feel vulnerable and fragile, it's hard to fend off the aggressive ideas of other people. If those around you (friends, family, healing professionals, etc.) are unsupportive, impatient, or derogatory, it will be tough to keep yourself on track. Always remember that the knowledge of the people around you (even the professionals) is limited by experience, research, and/ or training. Because of this, they do not have the last word. Their ideas are always subject to change and revision.

Alternatively, if you're lucky enough to have cheerleaders, it's important to allow them to support you but not to disrespect your own assessment of what is right for you and when. Sometimes, others will have terrific insights you haven't noticed; their input can be tremendously useful. However, they don't know what it's like to be you in this moment, so they don't always fully understand how or in what way to be helpful. You may be moving at exactly the right pace for you, for example. But when you make progress, the innocent excitement of others' responses may encourage you to move faster or more proactively. Following their advice can lead you right off track if it brings on feelings of being overwhelmed and puts you on their track, instead of your own.

> Filtering external sources offers an opportunity for self-trust and executive thinking. For every word that comes from an outside source, ask yourself if you agree with it or believe it's true. Offer yourself proof of why your answer has merit.

~~~~~~

Put in place some boundaries!

After trauma, it's normal to feel so raw that you just don't have the energy to keep up healthy boundaries. Or maybe your trauma demolished the boundaries you had or decimated your very perceptions of what boundaries are. In the aftermath of recovery, it's going to be necessary to rebuild them.

Some quick tips for doing this include:

- **Decide what kinds of boundaries are important to you.** Become very clear on what this looks like in terms of friends, family, colleagues, and neighbors, as well as physical, mental, and emotional parameters.

- **Recognize how the lack of boundaries affects your daily life.** Do you feel put upon, invaded, used, manipulated, or overwhelmed by the actions and behaviors of others? Identify where the boundaries are lacking, plus what needs to happen to install new ones.

- **Understand how a lack of boundaries triggers you and causes a reaction.** Notice your behavior in terms of isolation, anger, lashing out, hiding out, escaping, etc.

- **Imagine how your life would change if you had appropriate boundaries.** Tap into a very clear picture of what it would look, feel, and sound like to actively create the kind of healthy space in which you desire to live.

Making choices and taking actions are the cornerstones of shifting yourself from powerless to powerful. By reinstalling boundaries, you develop strength and the ability to take care of and protect yourself.

> Plan how to (re)instate the boundaries you desire. What will have to change for the boundaries to be installed? You'll have to speak up, move out, find strength within, hold the line, and demand change (in a nice way, or stronger if that's what it takes).

~~~~~

Hang with the right crew.

In healing, you can feel so desperate, desolate, isolated, and fragmented that you don't always make right or good decisions. Or perhaps you don't even make decisions; you do things by default. This can be hazardous to your recovery. If you want to heal, you must hoard your energy, rather than having it siphoned off or mutilated by the negative effects of others.

As a part of your healing process, it will help to raise your level of consciousness and use it in creating the world in which you live. An easy place to begin developing this skill is by being aware of the simple act of choosing whom you allow around you.

Take a look at the people with whom you surround yourself. Consider these questions:

- How do these people support or hinder my comfort level in being true to myself?

- How are these people good or bad/toxic for me?

- How do these people encourage/discourage my feeling good about me, my recovery, and the future?

If the answers are negative, it's time to begin thinking about how to change the energy that surrounds you.

> How conscious are you in choosing the people you spend time with? Take some time to evaluate the five to ten people you spend the most time with. Do they positively or negatively affect and influence you? For those who are negative, develop a plan to reduce the time you spend together. For those who are positive, make a plan to increase the time you spend together.

~~~~~~

Turn your back on the naysayers.

There will always be people who believe PTSD is a lifetime sentence. They are wrong. Many survivors are healing or have healed. They all experience a reduction in, or even elimination of, symptoms. You can too.

When you're faced with others' (or even your own) lack of belief, remind them:

- Zero research exists to prove that symptoms of PTSD are always permanent.

- A plethora of research suggests that PTSD symptoms can be reduced and/or eliminated.

If you want to have a little fun, the next time people you know claim that PTSD cannot be healed, share with them these other once-held erroneous beliefs:

- The world is flat.

- The sun revolves around the earth.

- The heavier the object, the faster it falls.

- No one can run a four-minute mile.

- The atom is the smallest particle.

- Space travel will never happen.

- There is no world market for personal computers.

- No one would want to see a movie in which the actors can be heard speaking.

- Nuclear energy is not obtainable.

- Air and rail travel are impossible.

There are several more examples to add to this list. Do your own research for quotes and articles about what people believed was true that was later proved wrong. The next time you or someone you know lacks faith in the possibility of your recovery, remind that person how many other "impossible" things have happened.

Be selfish.

Do you feel that it's not right for you to take a break from life to focus on yourself and your recovery? Or, do you receive messages from others that your healing journey is an inconvenience?

While it's true that there are certain life-must-go-on moments, situations, and responsibilities, it's also true that, right now, the most self*less* thing you can do for yourself and anyone else is to make healing a priority. It's a little like the directions you get on an airplane: In the event of an emergency, place the oxygen mask on yourself *before* you help the passenger sitting beside you.

When you feel okay, you are more adept, able, and equipped to help others or be a meaningful presence in their lives. Right this minute, the word *selfish* ceases to exist in any application to your healing process. Do what you need to, regardless of the noise it might create.

Healing is your opportunity to make yourself a priority. This is your time; take it.

> Practice being selfish: Identify an experience, choice, action, or activity that feels incredibly selfish, but that you know would be good for your healing process. Go into it full force today!

Use your willpower.

In the PTSD mindset, it's normal to swing from utter chaos to complete rigidity—and back!—several times a day. Either you throw all caution to the wind (chaos), or you determine to control every molecule in the universe (rigidity).

Having willpower can help you gain a little, or even a lot, more ability to choose which way you swing and when, or even to begin bringing yourself to a neutral place.

To develop willpower, imagine yourself as a person with one physical brain structure that shifts between two modes of operation: your Ideal Self and your Survivor Self. While it's reasonable and sometimes even necessary to shift immediately from one to the other without cognitive thought, it's also beneficial to recognize the different roles and how you can develop the conscious skill to choose one over the other.

> A simple way to develop willpower is to practice the art of deferral. The next time you want something, defer your gratification by waiting ten minutes before allowing yourself to have it. This simple action places you in the center of command, while simultaneously building a long-term skill set for control.

~~~~~~

Imagine change.

For a long time, you've been out of touch with what you really want below the surface of feeling better. You've also been out of touch with the many different parts of yourself. Probably, too, you've spent more time hating your symptoms than focusing on what makes recovery really matter.

In fact, when was the last time you thought deeply about how your life will change (in all the tiny and minute details that it will) when you emerge from the recovery process and into your whole new self?

When you become clear on what you want your life to look like in the future, you effectively train your brain to take actions to create that.

> List all of the things you'd like to change about you. Then, for a few moments, close your eyes and allow yourself to imagine that each of those individual details changes in exactly the way you'd like it to. Sit with this image and/or sensation for as long as feels right.

~~~~~~

There is more to be done in PTSD recovery than just eliminating symptoms.

There is a life to be recovered and a future to be lived. You have *survived*, meaning you "outlived" a traumatic event. Now you must outlive PTSD.

Thinking, expecting, and behaving oppositely can give you balance that allows you to find yourself in newly positive territory, with new and stimulating experiences that evolve your old perceptions and beliefs into a new lifestyle that supports the absence of PTSD.

Viktor Frankl wrote, "Everything can be taken from a man but one thing: the last of human freedoms—to choose one's attitude in any given set of circumstances, to choose one's own way."

If you continue to protect the negative beliefs and thoughts in your mind, you will always be a prisoner of the past. If you create a freedom in your mind—if you choose a different attitude, thought, focus, and belief—then you can take yourself one step closer to accomplishing how you want to rebuild your life after trauma.

> Identify one thought or belief that blocks your healing efforts. Now imagine acting as if the opposite were true. How would that positively change your daily experience? What healing outcomes might that open up?

~~~~~

Believe you're worth it.

Do you believe you deserve to heal from PTSD?

In his book *The Power of Intention,* Dr. Wayne Dyer writes, "If you don't believe that you're worthy of fulfilling your intentions...then you're creating an obstacle that will inhibit the flow of creative energy into your...life."

Trauma can strip you of all belief in your own deservedness. In fact, in a perverse way, trauma can make you believe you deserve the bad instead of the good. If this is happening to you, address it quickly before this belief derails your entire recovery effort.

When you feel (1) stuck, stalled, blocked, or set back; (2) despair that you'll never finish; or (3) like giving up, check in with how deeply you believe you deserve to succeed. Ask yourself this question:

• Do I believe my happiness, contentment, success, and good fortune are as deserved as that of everyone else?

If the answer is no, investigate: Why don't you believe this? Why is your self-respect at such a low level? What can you do to increase your belief in this area? Return to page 193 and put this belief through the limiting-beliefs debunking process.

Rate your belief "I deserve to heal" on a scale of 1 to 10 (10 being "I believe it 100 percent!"). If you are anywhere below a 10, pause in your recovery and identify (1) what it would take to move up one notch and (2) how you can do that and who can help. Keep going until you reach 10.

If your answers are all yes, but you still feel stalled, revisit each question and ask, "What might make the answer be no?" In the discoveries you make will lie the seeds of the block that's holding you back below the surface.

Always remember: You have enormous healing potential; the goal is learning to access it. You can do this. Dig deep. I believe in you!

ACKNOWLEDGMENTS

By the time I finish writing a book, I'm always amazed by how the original idea has evolved: What began as a small concept with a zillion fragments somehow transforms into a cohesive and marvelous whole. This is part of the fun of writing. While you're not looking (or, busy looking elsewhere), magic happens.

The magic of this book began with an email from my first editor, Amber Guetebier, inquiring whether I had an idea for a book. Yes, I said, as a matter of fact I did. For several years I'd been writing a Healing Thought of the Day for the HealMyPTSD.com audience. Many survivors had expressed the desire to have the thoughts collected in a book. Amber liked the suggestion, and with her help, the fantastic team at Conari came on board. Great thanks to the entire Conari family, who saw the potential of my idea and helped cast the spell that created this book, including Jane Hagaman and Charles Hutchinson. Special thanks goes to my second editor, Caroline Pincus, for so graciously stepping in and appreciating the book's intention, and Eryn Carter—the only marketing professional I know with a degree in social media—for helping put the "abracadabra" in materializing this book in the world.

Without Sheila Levine at Levine Samuel, LLP, I wouldn't know my way around a contract. Much thanks goes to her for being a great friend and mentor, and for continually making sure that I know what to sign and when. Thanks also to my assistant, Maria Dal Pra, for conjuring the first compilation of healing thoughts.

All of the books I write begin with a desire to be helpful, which means that the trauma survivor community of which I am a part is a constant source of inspiration, illumination, and motivation. Thanks to all colleagues for the creative time we've spent in the trenches swapping suggestions for how to be even more effective at helping survivors heal. Special thanks to every survivor with whom I have interacted, from private and group clients to those who have reached out via my website, email, social media, and the Heal My PTSD forum. By sharing, in conversations, your thoughts, dreams, and struggles, you allow us to explore what can lead to healing resolutions. By implementing my sometimes crazy-sounding suggestions, you've all helped build a sandbox in which we refine ideas and see what works. We're truly all in this together.

To create this book, I started with a fresh approach, not only to write new healing thoughts, but in an expanded version that also pairs each thought with an action. My top four supporters—Eileen and Gary Rosenthal, John Lawrence, and Bret Rosenthal—tolerated countless hours of healing thought ideas, theories, explanations, and exercises as I tried them out on an audience during lunches, dinners, vacations, and walks on the beach. For having the patience to listen and the generosity to also be deeply interested and offer feedback, you have my enormous gratitude. And, of course, always my love.

ABOUT THE AUTHOR

Michele Rosenthal is an award-winning PTSD blogger, post-trauma coach, and former faculty member of the Clinical Development Institute for Timberline Knolls Residential Treatment Center. She's the author of *Before the World Intruded: Conquering the Past and Creating the Future* (selected as a finalist for the Books For A Better Life Award, Next Generation Indie Book Award, and the International Book Award), and *Your Life After Trauma: Powerful Practices to Reclaim Your Identity* (W. W. Norton).

When she's not researching, studying, or writing about how to overcome the effects of trauma, Michele is out enjoying the benefits of being PTSD-free by dancing salsa or Argentine tango, or taking a long walk on the beach near her home in South Florida.

Visit the author's website at www.mytraumacoach.com.

FURTHER RESOURCES

During my PTSD recovery and afterward, I participated in PTSD-specific forums to find other like-minded souls. What I often found were angry, antagonistic, manipulative, and disrespectful people, which made for toxic groups. In a bid to create a PTSD community that is positive, supportive, judgment-free, creative, open, and compassionate, I accepted an invitation from the CEO of HealthUnlocked.com to found the Heal My PTSD forum on their site. With the help of some terrific administrators from the Heal My PTSD community, we have created a forum that glows with information, ideas, and camaraderie. Join us in this free, secure, and, if you choose, anonymous space: HealthUnlocked.com/HealMyPTSD.

Sometimes you just need a good old-fashioned list to get you focused, on track, and in motion. The following resources represent some of my favorite choices for trauma- and PTSD-related books and podcasts.

BOOKS

Amen, Daniel. *Change Your Brain, Change Your Life: The Breakthrough Program for Conquering Anxiety, Depression, Obsessiveness, Anger, and Impulsiveness.* Goshen: Harmony, 1999.

Brach, Tara. *Radical Acceptance: Embracing Your Life with the Heart of a Buddha.* New York: Bantam, 2004.

Hanson, Rick. *Hardwiring Happiness: The New Brain Science of Contentment, Calm, and Confidence.* Goshen: Harmony, 2013.

Herman, Judith. *Trauma and Recovery: The Aftermath of Violence—from Domestic Abuse to Political Terror,* reprint edition. New York: Basic Books, 1997.

Kabat-Zinn, Jon. *Full Catastrophe Living: Using the Wisdom of Your Body and Mind to Face Stress, Pain, and Illness,* revised updated edition. New York: Bantam, 2013.

Levine, Peter A. *In an Unspoken Voice: How the Body Releases Trauma and Restores Goodness.* Berkeley: North Atlantic Books, 2010.

Levine, Peter A. *Waking the Tiger: Healing Trauma.* Berkeley: North Atlantic Books, 1997.

Naparstek, Belleruth. *Invisible Heroes: Survivors of Trauma and How They Heal.* New York: Bantam, 2005.

Rosenbloom, Dena, and Mary Beth Williams. *Life After Trauma: A Workbook for Healing,* second edition. New York: The Guilford Press, 2010.

Rosenthal, Michele. *Before the World Intruded: Conquering the Past and Creating the Future, A Memoir.* Palm Beach Gardens: Your Life After Trauma, 2012.

Rosenthal, Michele. *Your Life After Trauma: Powerful Practices to Reclaim Your Identity.* New York: W. W. Norton, 2015.

Rothschild, Babette. *8 Keys to Safe Trauma Recovery: Take-Charge Strategies to Empower Your Healing.* New York: W. W. Norton, 2010.

Rothschild, Babette. *The Body Remembers: The Psychophysiology of Trauma and Trauma Treatment.* New York: W. W. Norton, 2000.

Scaer, Robert. *8 Keys to Brain-Body Balance.* New York: W. W. Norton, 2012.

Scaer, Robert. *The Body Bears the Burden: Trauma, Dissociation, and Disease.* New York: Routledge, 2014.

Scaer, Robert. *The Trauma Spectrum: Hidden Wounds and Human Resiliency.* New York: W. W. Norton, 2005.

Schiraldi, Glenn. *The Post-Traumatic Stress Disorder Sourcebook: A Guide to Healing, Recovery, and Growth.* New York: McGraw-Hill, 2009.

Van der Kolk, Bessel. *The Body Keeps the Score: Brain, Mind, and Body in the Healing of Trauma.* New York: Viking, 2014.

Walker, Pete. *Complex PTSD: From Surviving to Thriving: A Guide and Map for Recovering from Childhood Trauma.* Charleston, SC: CreateSpace Independent Publishing Platform, 2013.

Williams, Mary Beth, and Soili Poijula. *The PTSD Workbook: Simple, Effective Techniques for Overcoming Traumatic Stress Symptoms,* third edition. Oakland: New Harbinger Publications, 2016.

APPENDIX

DO I HAVE PTSD?

Whether or not you have a clinical PTSD diagnosis (applied by a licensed health-care professional), this book is designed to help you learn how to improve your anxiety-coping skills; increase your knowledge about how the past affects your present; and inspire you to implement changes in what you think, how you behave, and the way you feel.

If you desire certainty about the clinical presence of PTSD, the following information will advance your knowledge and allow you to picture the diagnostic criteria as they apply to you. If this information aligns with experience and/or presentation of symptoms, it is possible that you have PTSD. Receiving a professional diagnosis would be your next step and can be accomplished by meeting with a mental health professional trained in the diagnostic criteria of post-traumatic stress disorder.

PTSD CRITERIA

The following elements are recognized as PTSD symptoms when they occur naturally (that is, not induced by substances or a medical condition); have existed for more than four weeks; and cause significant dysfunction in your social, personal, and/or professional areas of life.

- **Exposure:** Experience of a situation that threatens death, injury, or sexual violence in ways that you directly experienced the event, witnessed it in person as it happened to someone else, heard about the event happening to a close family member or friend, or experienced repeated and extreme interaction with details of the traumatic event (e.g., first responders).

- **Re-experiencing:** Recurrent intrusive memories and thoughts about the event, dreams, and nightmares with (thematically) related content, reactions (i.e., flashbacks) in which it feels as though the event is happening in real time, enormous psychological and/or physiological distress brought on by external or internal cues that resemble aspects of the trauma.

- **Avoidance:** Persistent circumvention of both internal and external cues that resemble traumatic content, including thoughts, memories, locations, people, and sensory stimulation.

- **Alterations:** Changes in cognition or mood, as evidenced by amnesia for an important aspect of the trauma; exaggerated and frequent negative beliefs about oneself, others, and the world; distorted ideas about the cause or consequences related to the trauma that lead to blaming yourself or others; consistent negative emotional perspective; lessened interest and participation in activities that previously engendered good feelings; a sense of detachment from yourself or others; long-term inability to genuinely express positive emotions.

- **Arousal:** Increase in the following behaviors subsequent to the traumatic event, including irritability, anger/rage, self-destructive tendencies, hypervigilance, exaggerated startle response, concentration issues, and sleep disturbances.

While many aspects of PTSD may occur immediately following a trauma, some people experience delayed expression: The full spectrum of diagnosable criteria develops more than six months following the trauma. In addition to the symptoms here outlined, many survivors also experience dissociative symptoms, which include depersonalization (feeling detached from your mind and/or body) and derealization (feeling that the world and your surroundings are unreal).

PTSD SELF-TEST

For each statement, circle the answer that applies to you:

1. I have experienced or been exposed to a traumatic event. Yes/No

2. During the traumatic event, I experienced/witnessed serious injury or death, or the threat of injury or death. Yes/No

3. During the traumatic event, I felt intense fear, helplessness, and/or horror. Yes/No

4. I regularly experience intrusive thoughts or images about the traumatic event. Yes/No

5. I experience moments that feel as if I'm reliving the event or that it is happening again in real time. Yes/No

6. I have recurrent nightmares/distressing dreams about the traumatic event. Yes/No

7. I feel intense physical and/or emotional distress when something reminds me of the traumatic event, whether it's something I think about or see. Yes/No

8. I do my best to avoid thoughts, feelings, or conversations that remind me of the traumatic event. Yes/No

9. I do my best to avoid activities, people, or places that remind me of the traumatic event. Yes/No

10. I have memory gaps or find myself unable to remember something important about the traumatic event. Yes/No

11. Since the trauma occurred, I feel less interested in activities or hobbies that I used to enjoy. Yes/No

12. Since the trauma occurred, I feel distant from other people and/or have difficulty trusting them. Yes/No

13. Since the trauma occurred, I have difficulty regulating, experiencing, or showing emotions. Yes/No

14. I have a consistently negative mood in which I experience persistent negative beliefs about myself, have difficulty feeling positive emotions, and feel very negative about my future,

including feeling it will not be "normal" or that I won't have a career, marriage, children, or a normally expected life span. Yes/No

15. Since the traumatic event occurred, I have difficulty falling and/or staying asleep. Yes/No

16. Since the traumatic event occurred, I feel irritable and/or have outbursts of anger. Yes/No

17. Since the traumatic event occurred, I have difficulty concentrating. Yes/No

18. Since the traumatic event occurred, I feel guilty because others died or were hurt during the event, but I survived. Yes/No

19. Since the traumatic event occurred, I often feel jumpy or startle easily. Yes/No

20. Since the traumatic event occurred, I often feel hypervigilant (i.e., I am constantly feeling and acting ready for any kind of danger or threat). Yes/No

21. My experience of the symptoms recognized above has lasted for longer than one month. Yes/No

22. The symptoms I experience interfere with normal routines, work or school, and/or social activities. Yes/No

SCORING:

Add up the number of "Yes" answers:

- 1–3 = Few symptoms of PTSD
- 4–9 = PTSD likely
- 10+ = You display many symptoms of PTSD.

If you believe you have PTSD, share this self-test with your doctor or other healing professional. This is not a diagnosis. Only a qualified mental health professional can make a diagnosis of PTSD.

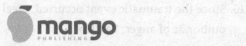